MW01628503

IMAGES *and* TESTIMONIES *of*
THE LIVING CHRIST

Cover image *Light of the World* © 2006 Greg Olsen. Courtesy of Greg Olsen Art, LLC. For print information call 1-208-888-2585 or go to www.gregolsenart.com. Back cover image: *Christ Walking on the Waters* by Julius Von Klever. Courtesy of Sotheby's Picture Library. For information on art prints go to www.foveditions.com

Cover and book design by Jessica A. Warner © 2006 by Covenant Communications, Inc.

Published by Covenant Communications, Inc.
American Fork, Utah

Printed in China
First Printing: September 2006

12 11 10 09 08 07 06 10 9 8 7 6 5 4 3 2 1

ISBN 1-59811-101-9

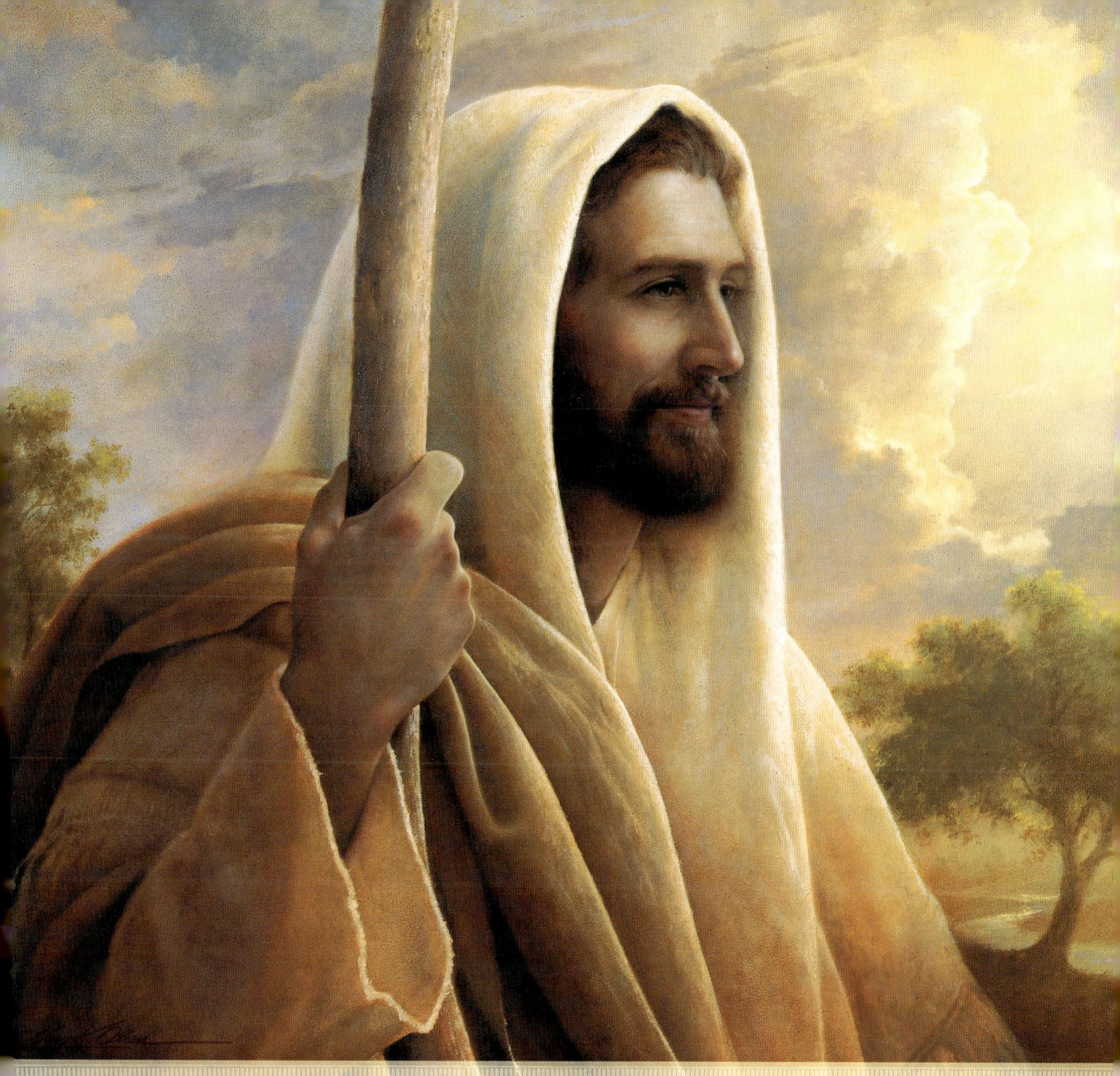

IMAGES *and* TESTIMONIES *of*

THE LIVING CHRIST

TABLE *of* CONTENTS

OF HIM WE TESTIFY 2

LIGHT OF THE WORLD 24

COME, FOLLOW ME 38

HIS ATONING SACRIFICE 58

OUR RESURRECTED LORD 82

MY WORK AND MY GLORY 98

ART CREDITS 117

OF HIM WE TESTIFY

Towering above all mankind stands Jesus the Christ, the King of glory, the unblemished Messiah, the Lord Emmanuel. . . . He is our King, our Lord, our Master, **THE LIVING CHRIST,** *who stands on the right hand of His Father. He lives! He lives, resplendent and wonderful, the living Son of the living God.*

President Gordon B. Hinckley, *Ensign*, May 1996

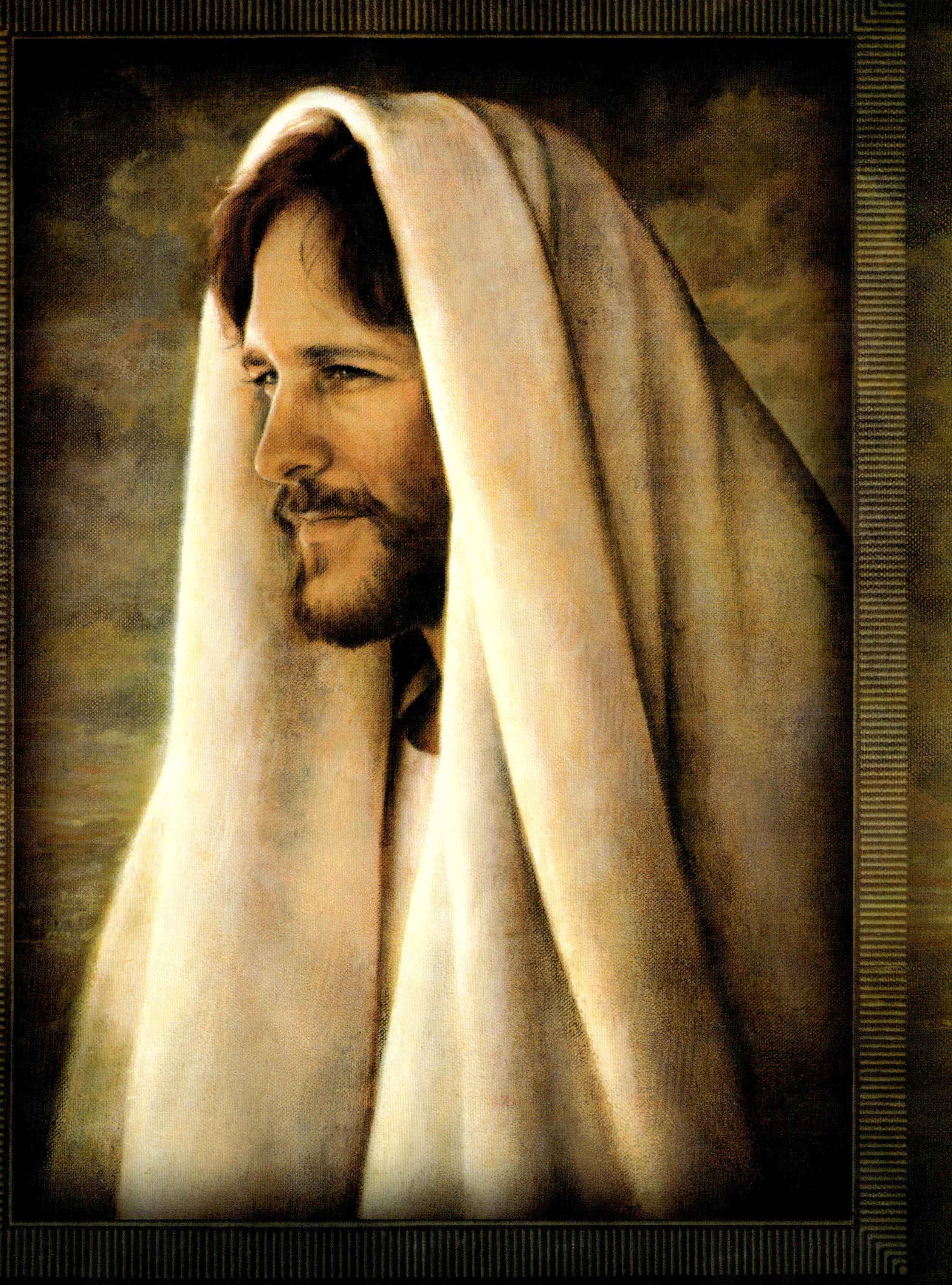

As pertaining to Jesus Christ, I testify that he is the Son of the Living God and was crucified for the sins of the world. He is our Lord, our God, and our King. This I know of myself independent of any other person.

I am one of his witnesses, and in a coming day I shall feel the nail marks in his hands and in his feet and shall wet his feet with my tears.

But I shall not know any better then than I know now that he is God's Almighty Son, that he is our Savior and Redeemer, and that salvation comes in and through his atoning blood and in no other way.

Bruce R. McConkie, "The Purifying Power of Gethsemane," *Ensign*, May 1985, 11

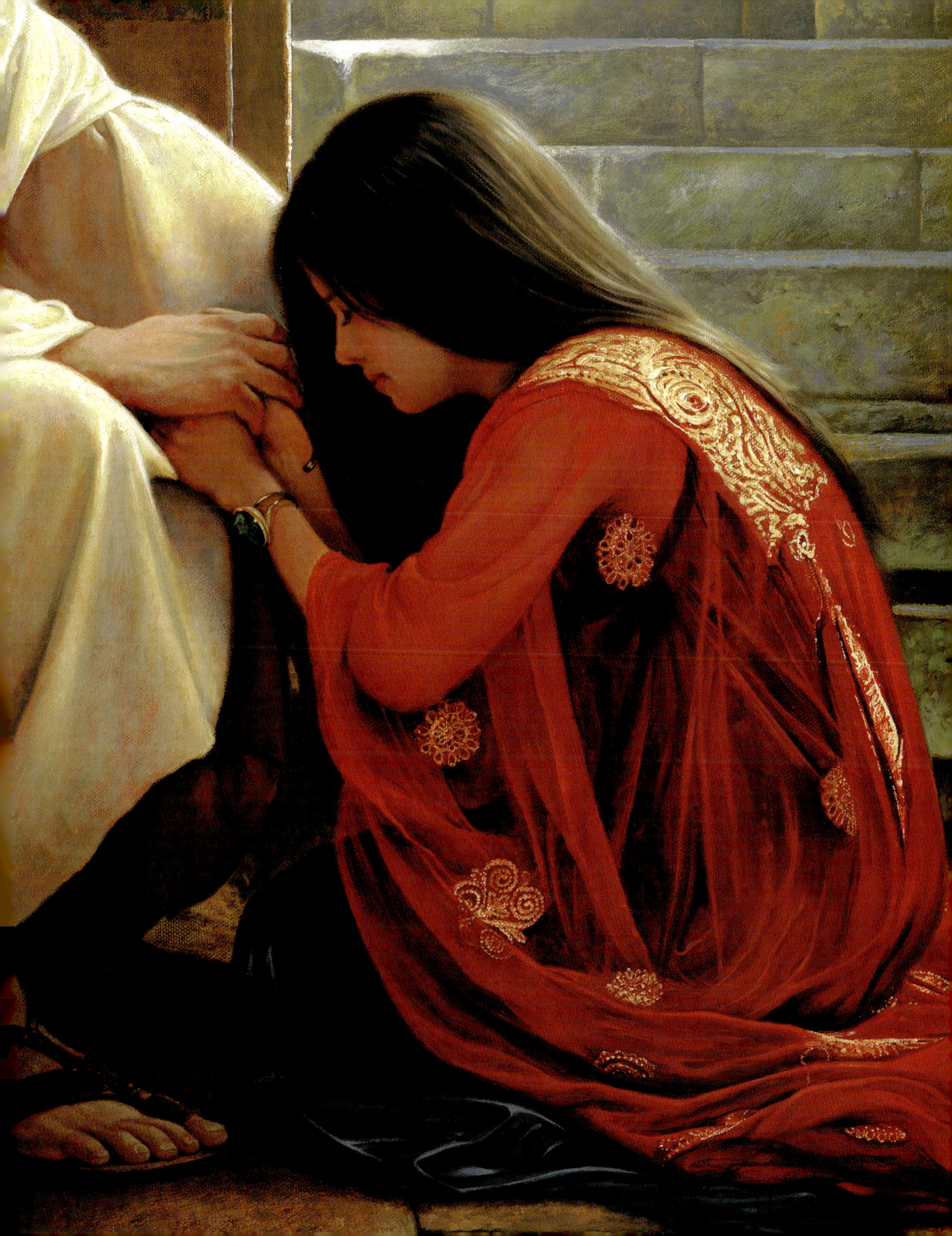

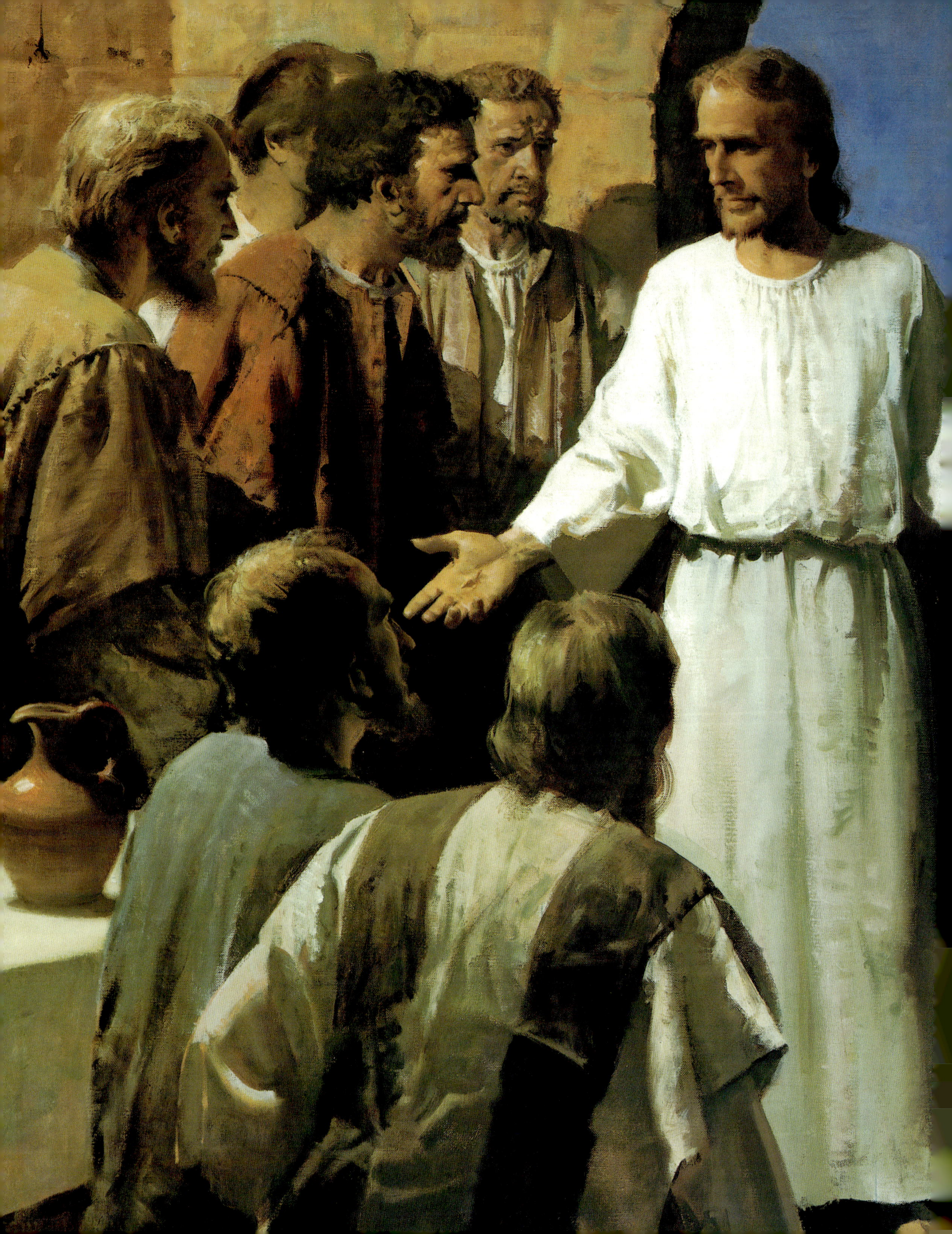

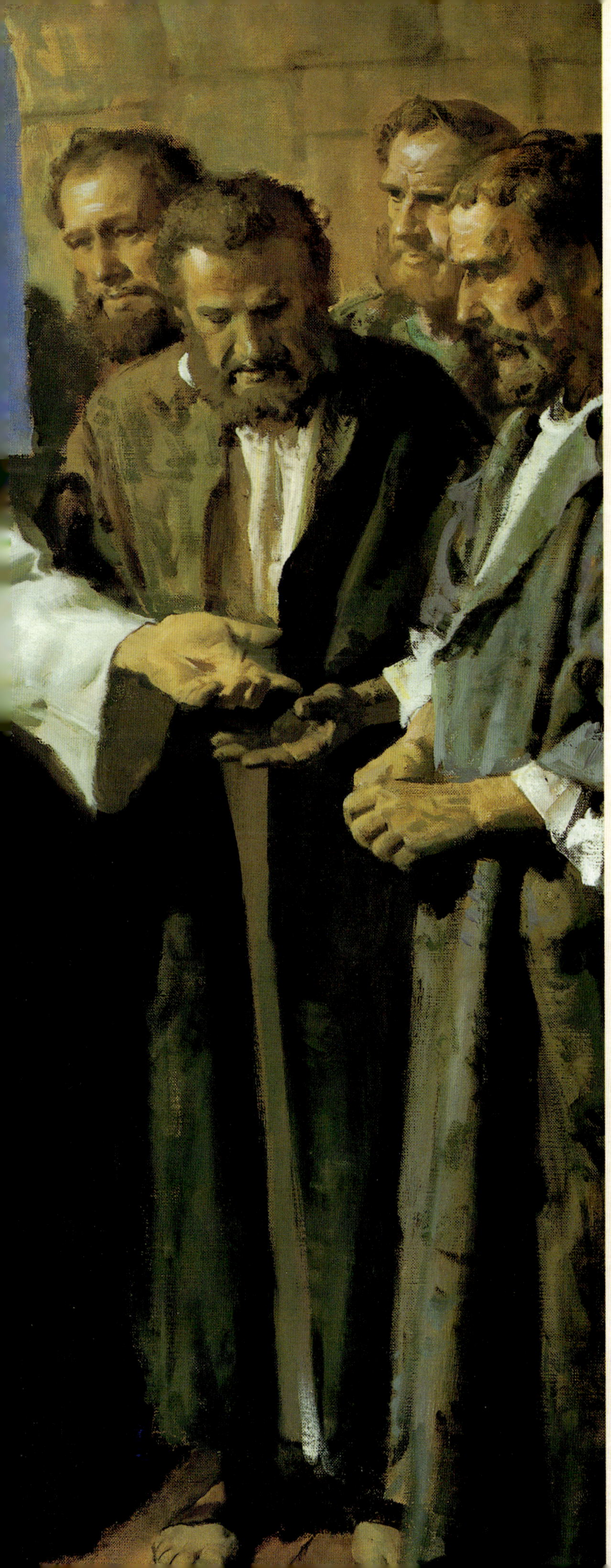

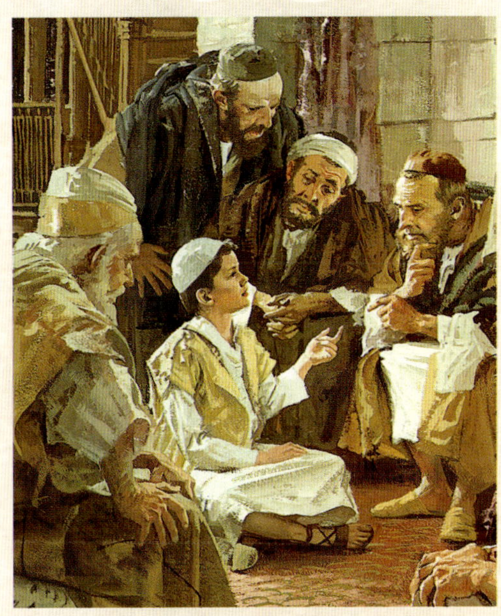

HUMAN HISTORY HAS NO ULTIMATE meaning without Christ. Christ is the verification of God's purposes for mankind, of the meaning of this life; He is the assurance of life to come. To accept him is an act drenched in meaning and significance. To testify of him is to testify to the reality of all that matters.

Neal A. Maxwell, "Our Acceptance of Christ," *Ensign*, June 1984, 69

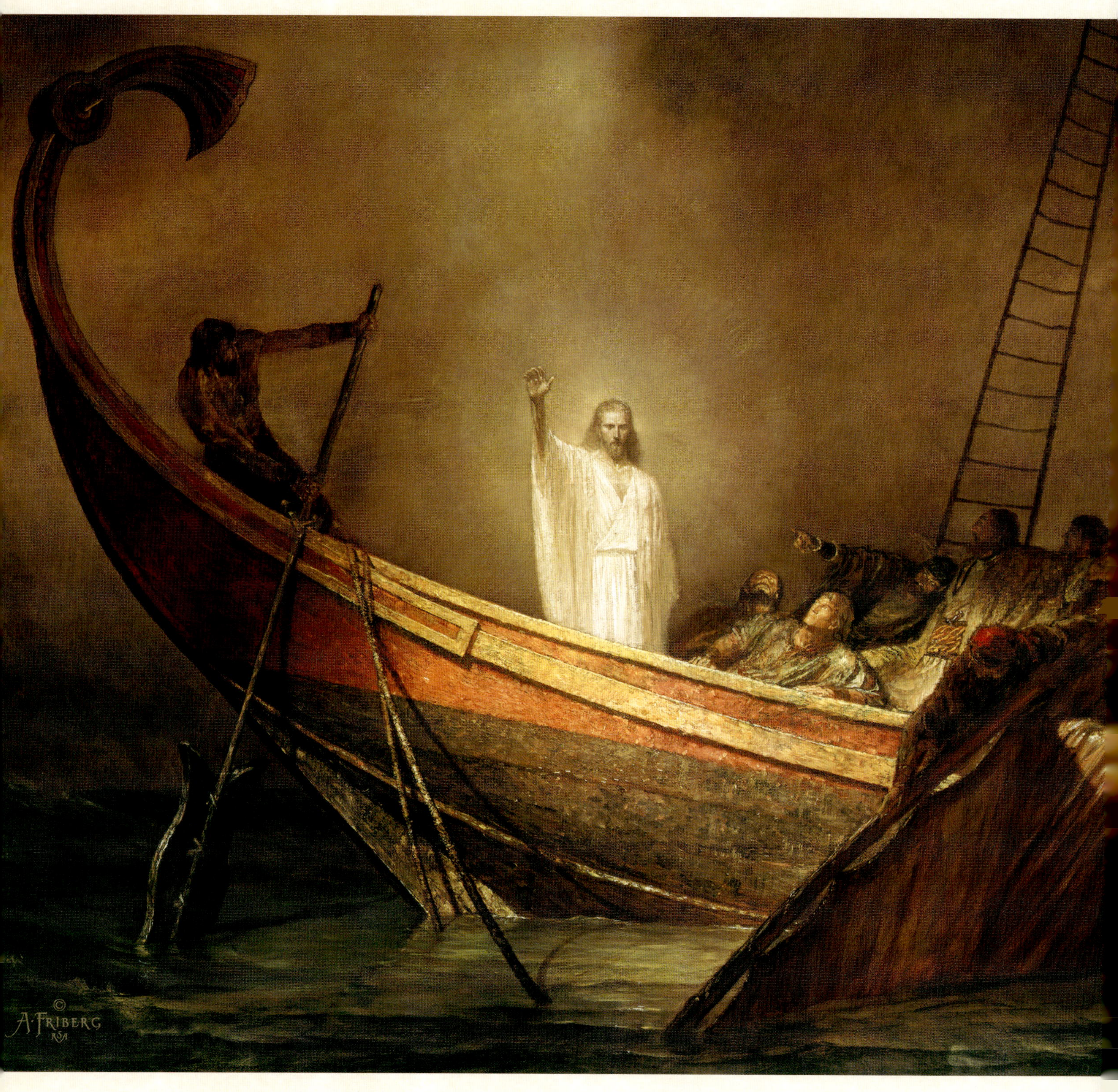
©
A·FRIBERG
RSA

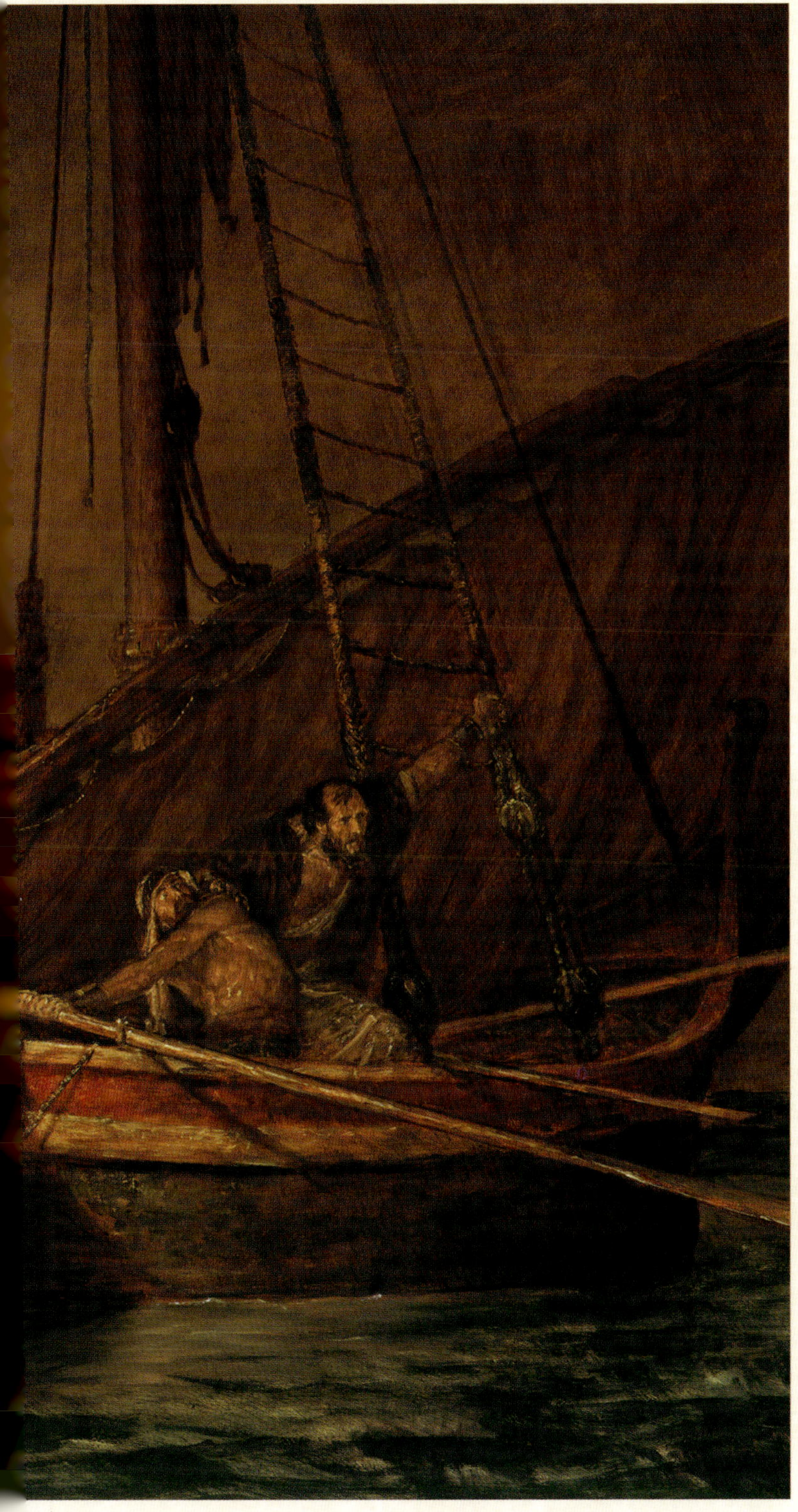

And he arose, and rebuked the wind,
and said unto the sea, Peace, be still.
And the wind ceased, and there was a great calm.

Mark 4:39

EACH OF US HAS TO RECEIVE OUR OWN witness concerning Jesus as the Christ. We cannot get it secondhand from someone else. I believe that a testimony of our Redeemer comes from a divine source, as a spiritual gift. Such a heaven-sent witness gives us a sacred inner peace and strength, even though we live in a world of turmoil and temptation. It gives us the power to become disciples of the Christ. As one who has sought such a witness, I would like to set my seal upon the testimony that has come to me of the reality of the Lord Jesus Christ.

James E. Faust, "A Testimony of Christ," *Ensign*, March 2005, 3

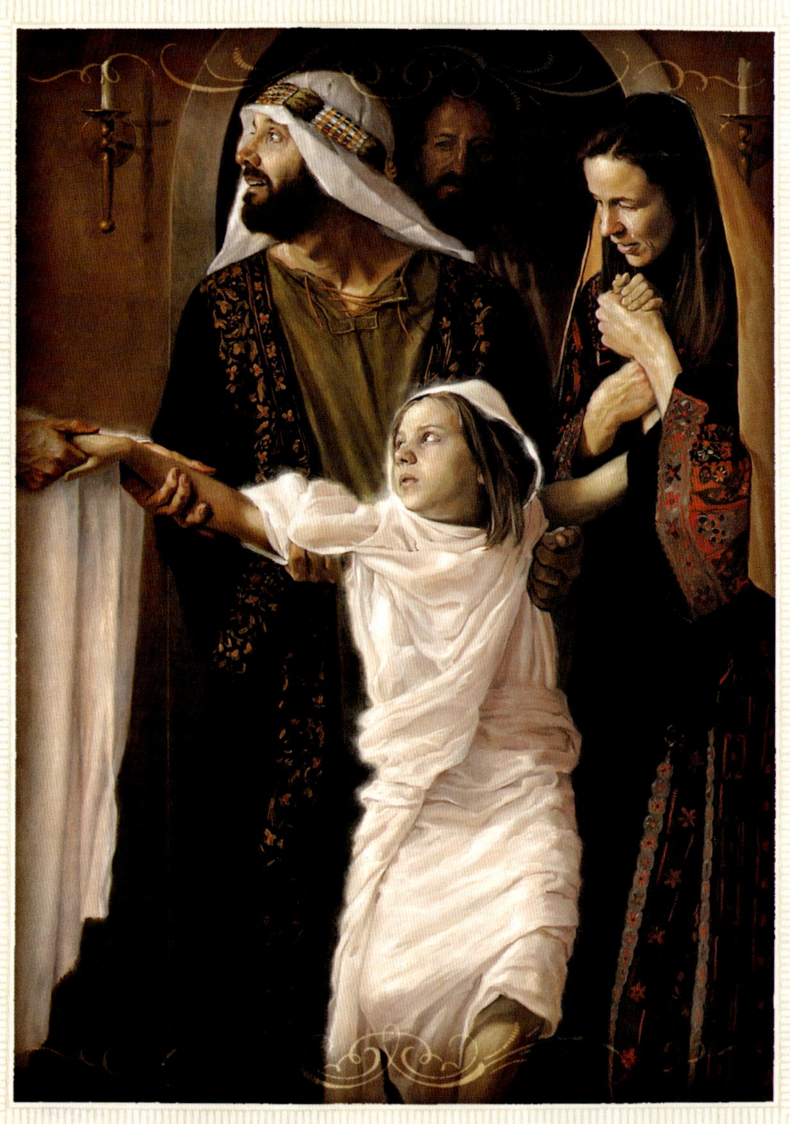

FOR I KNOW THAT MY REDEEMER LIVETH, and that he shall stand at the latter day upon the earth:

And though after my skin worms destroy this body, yet in my flesh shall I see God.

Job 19:25–26

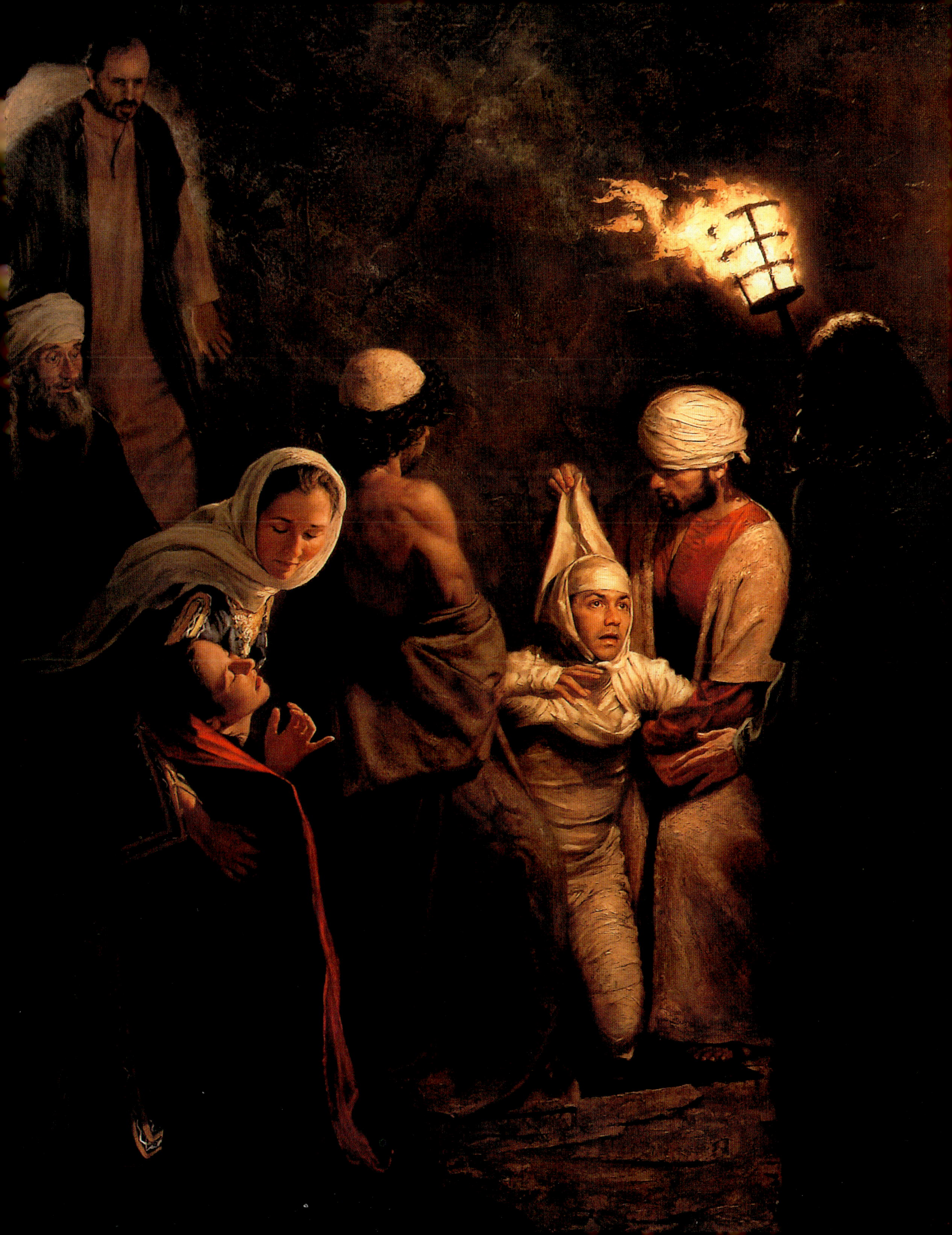

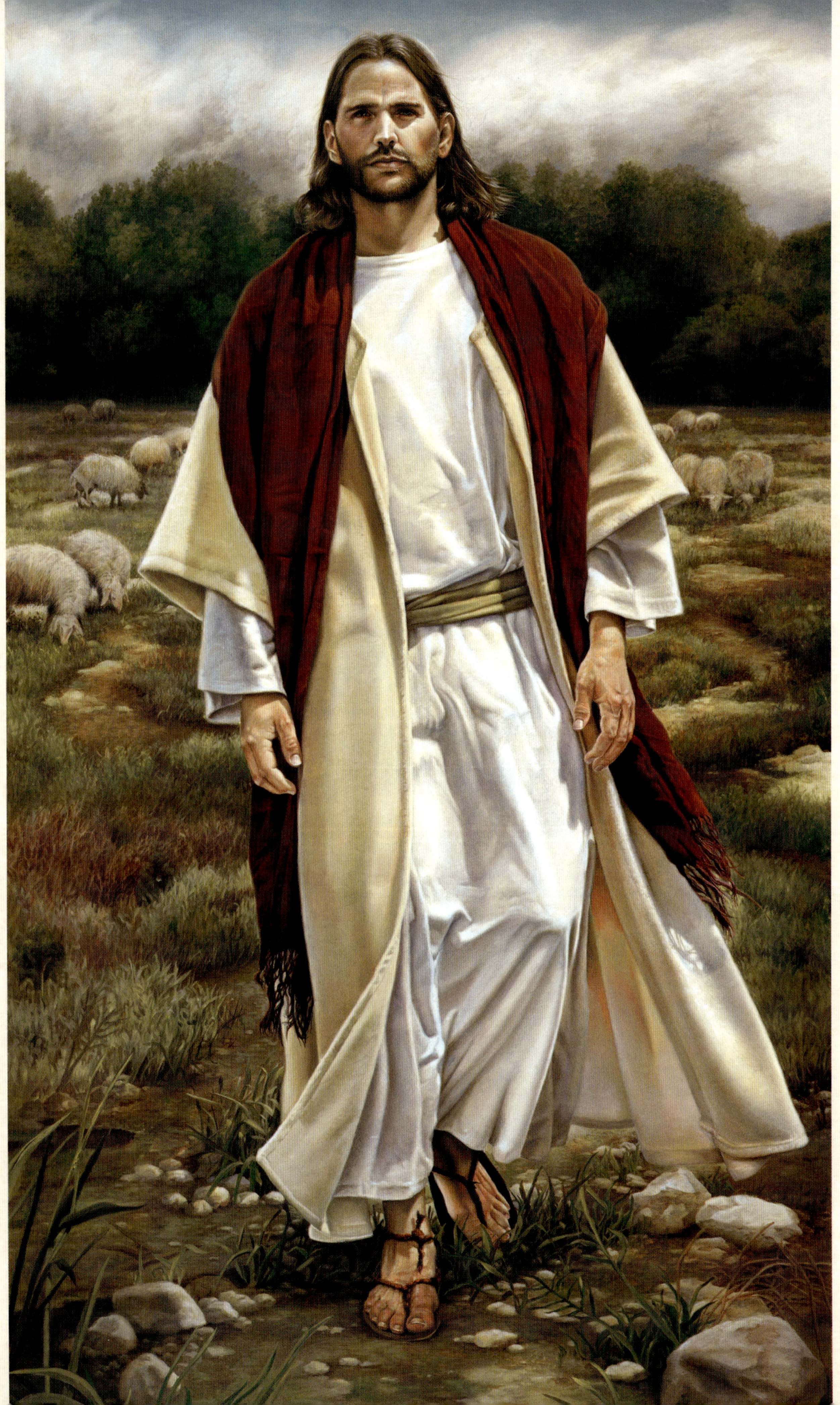

We need not visit the Holy Land to feel him close to us. We need not walk by the shores of Galilee or among the Judean hills to walk where Jesus walked.

In a very real sense, all can walk where Jesus walked when, with his words on our lips, his spirit in our hearts, and his teachings in our lives, we journey through mortality . . .

As you and I walk the pathway Jesus walked, let us listen for the sound of sandaled feet. Let us reach out for the Carpenter's hand. Then we shall come to know him.

Thomas S. Monson, "The Paths Jesus Walked," *Ensign*, May 1974, 48

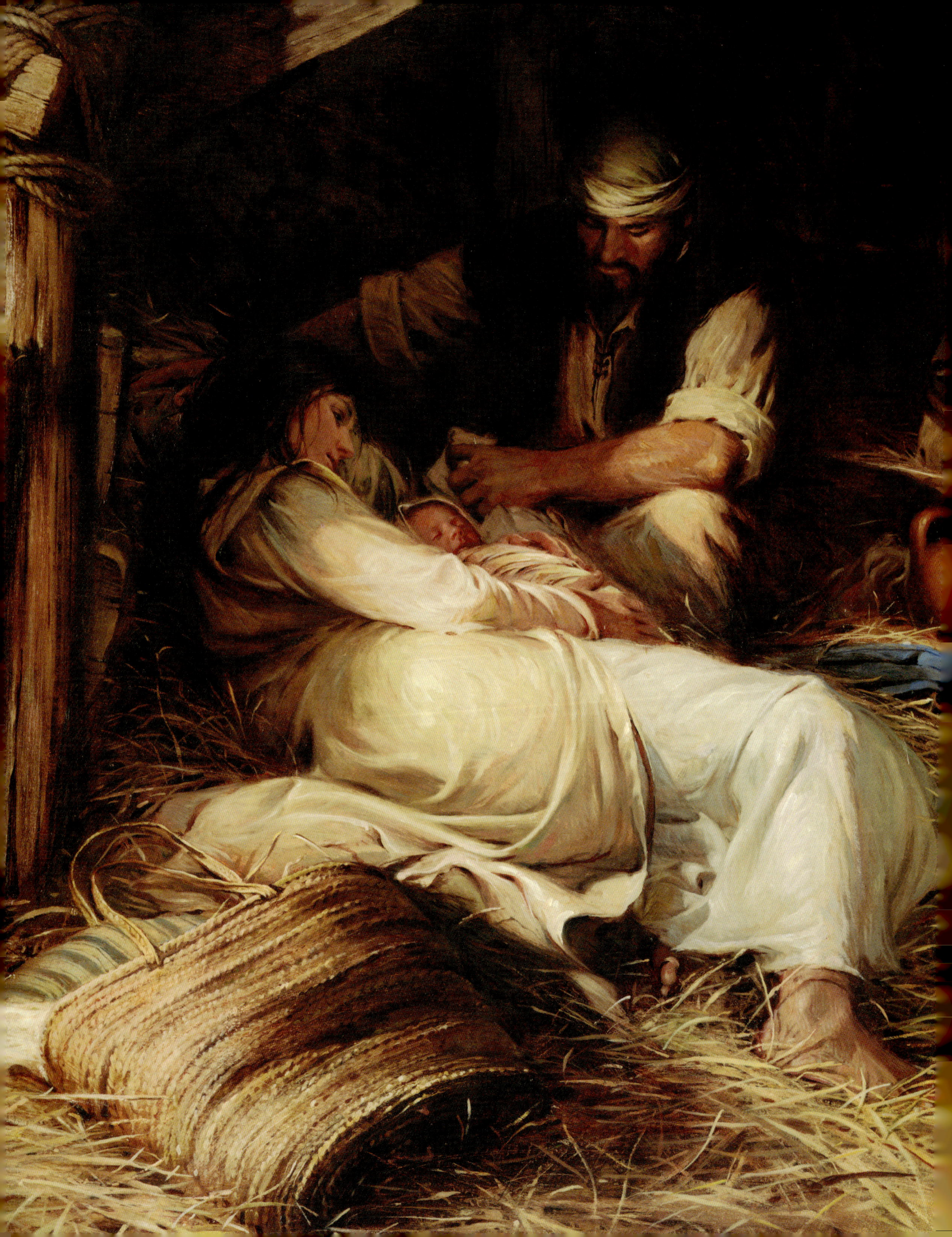

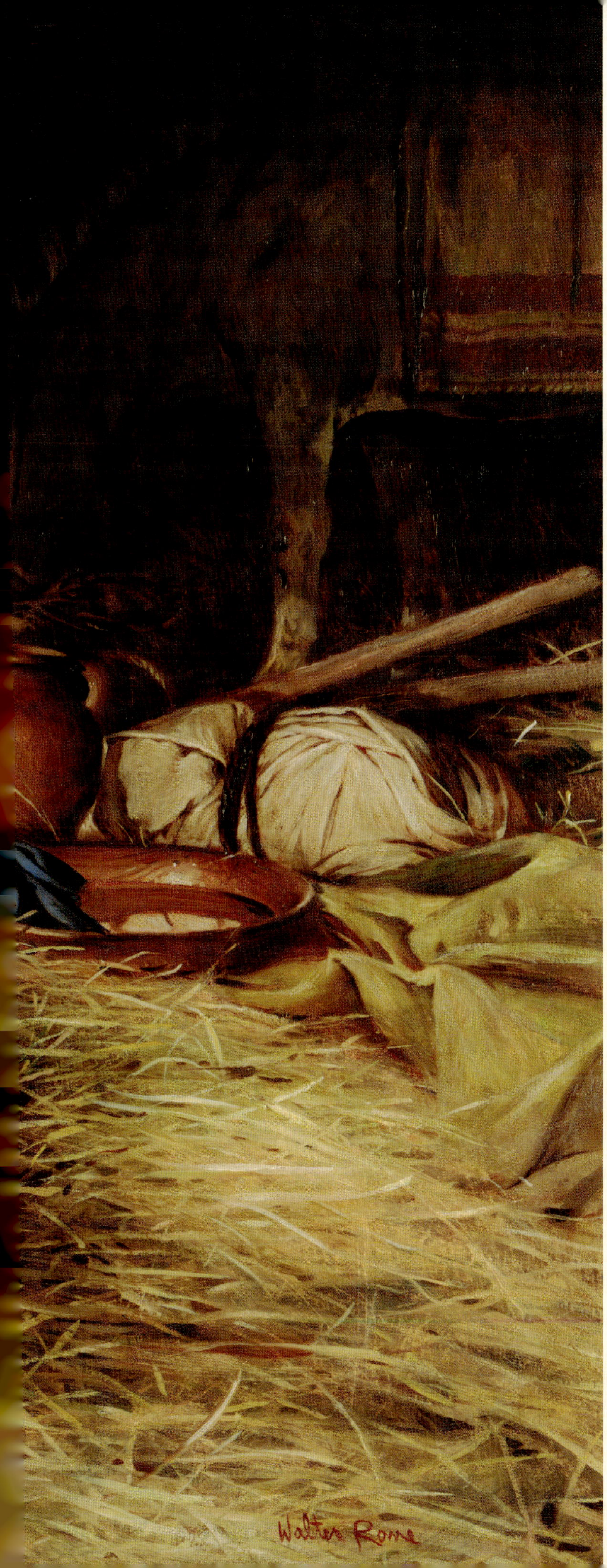

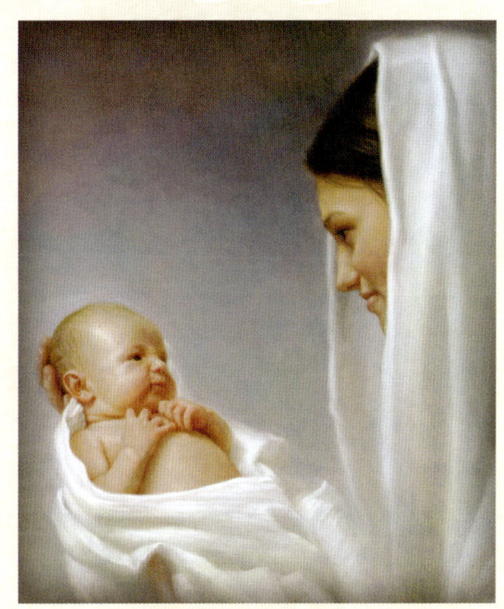

THE CRUX OF OUR MESSAGE IS THAT Jesus of Nazareth is Christ the Lord, the Redeemer of all mankind, the Savior of the Christians and the Messiah of the Jews. We affirm most solemnly that this same Jesus was the literal begotten Son of God, born of Mary, and that without him there is no Savior.

Mark E. Petersen, "Hear Ye Him!" *Ensign*, November 1975, 63

We discover He is more than the babe in Bethlehem, more than the carpenter's son, more than the greatest teacher ever to live. We come to know Him as the Son of God. He never fashioned a statue, painted a picture, wrote a poem, or led an army. He never wore a crown or held a scepter or threw around His shoulder a purple robe. His forgiveness was unbounded, His patience inexhaustible, His courage without limit.

Jesus changed men. He changed their habits, their opinions, their ambitions. He changed their tempers, their dispositions, their natures. He changed men's hearts.

Thomas S. Monson, "The Paths Jesus Walked," *Ensign*, September 1992, 2

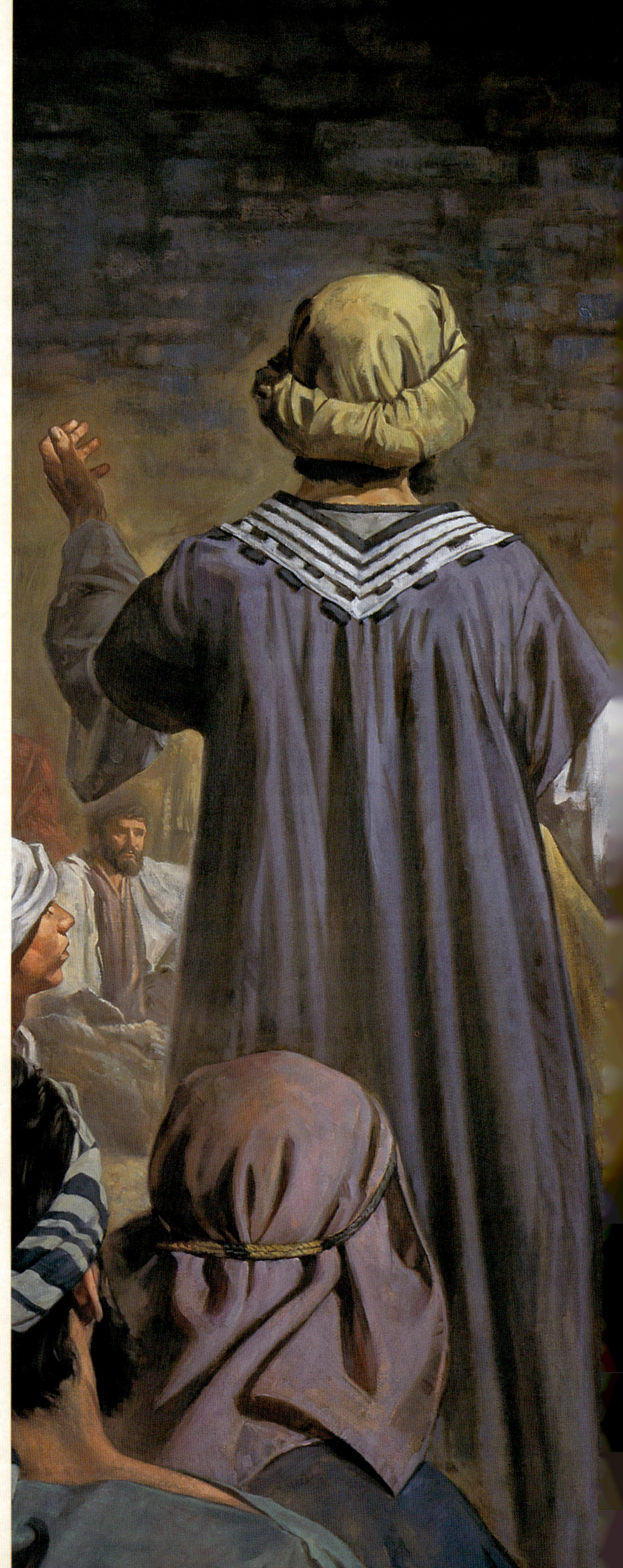

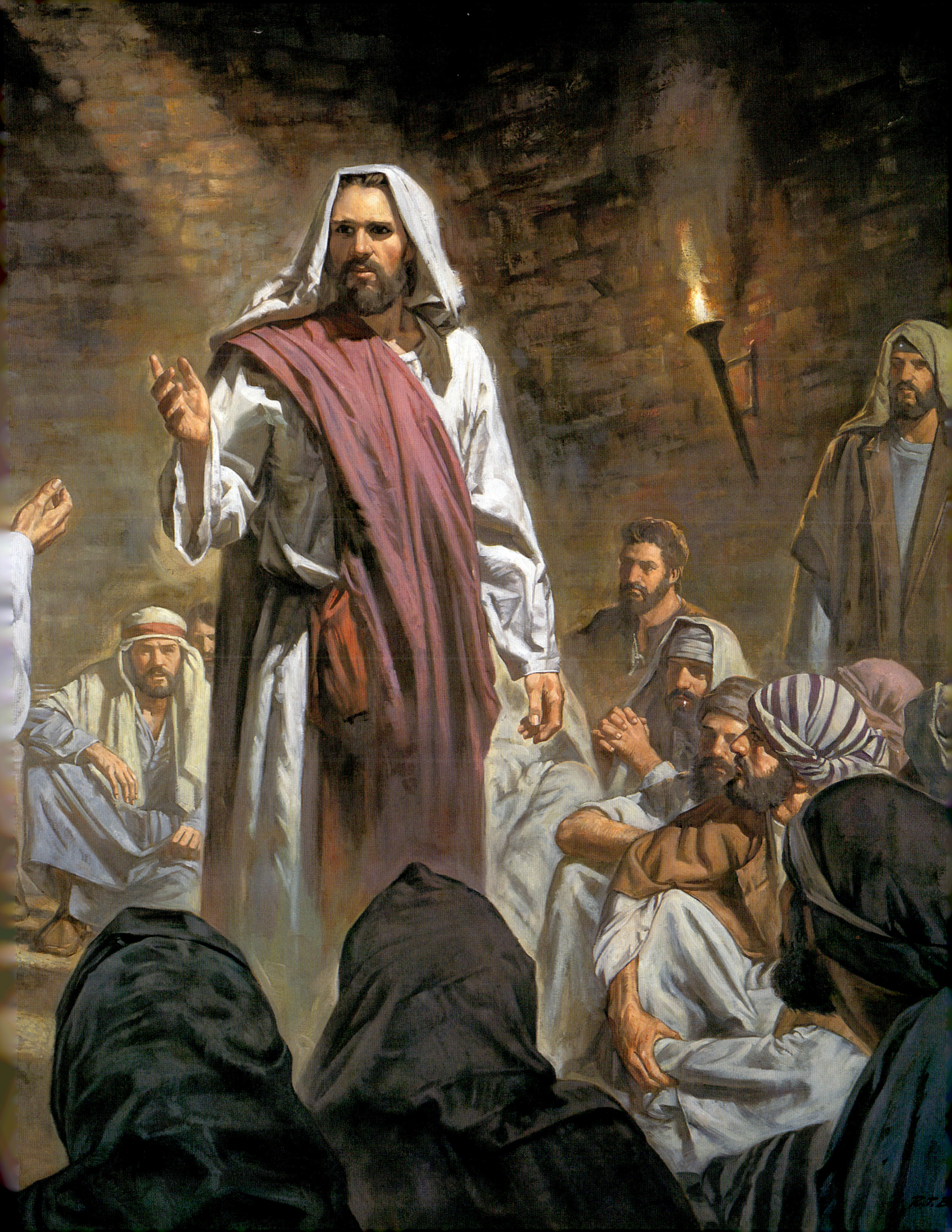

THIS IS HIS GOSPEL. HE STANDS AT THE head—holy, divine, supreme, full of power, majesty, grace, and truth. He lived for us, and He died for us, because He loves us. I love Him more deeply and powerfully than I can find words to express. He is my Lord, my Savior, my Redeemer, and my friend. I know that Jesus Christ is the Son of God our Eternal Father. He lives and directs His Church today through His prophet and His Apostles. His great work will continue to roll forth until it fills the whole earth.

M. Russell Ballard, "Special Witnesses of Christ," *Ensign*, April 2001, 4

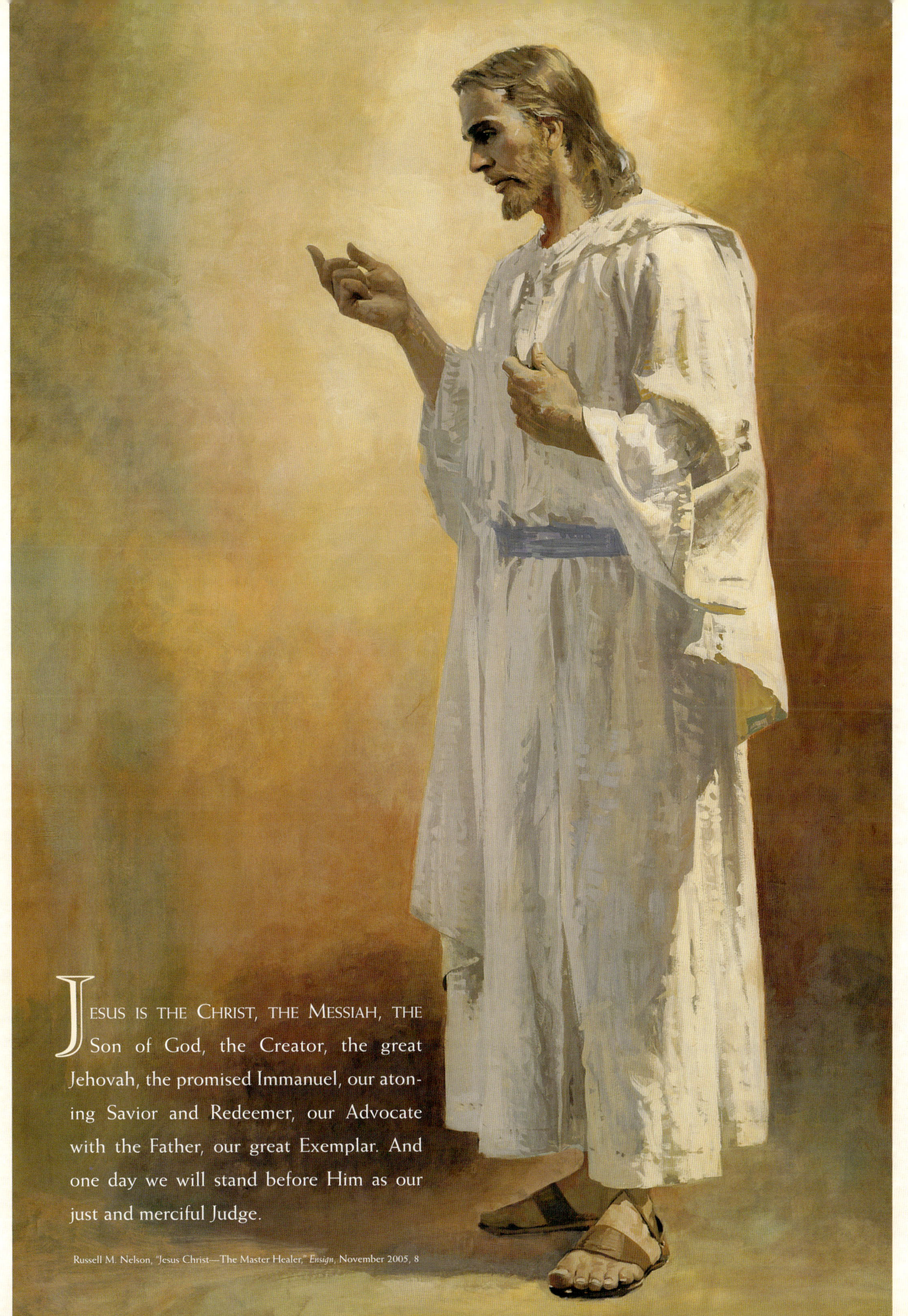
Jesus is the Christ, the Messiah, the Son of God, the Creator, the great Jehovah, the promised Immanuel, our atoning Savior and Redeemer, our Advocate with the Father, our great Exemplar. And one day we will stand before Him as our just and merciful Judge.
Russell M. Nelson, "Jesus Christ—The Master Healer," *Ensign*, November 2005, 8

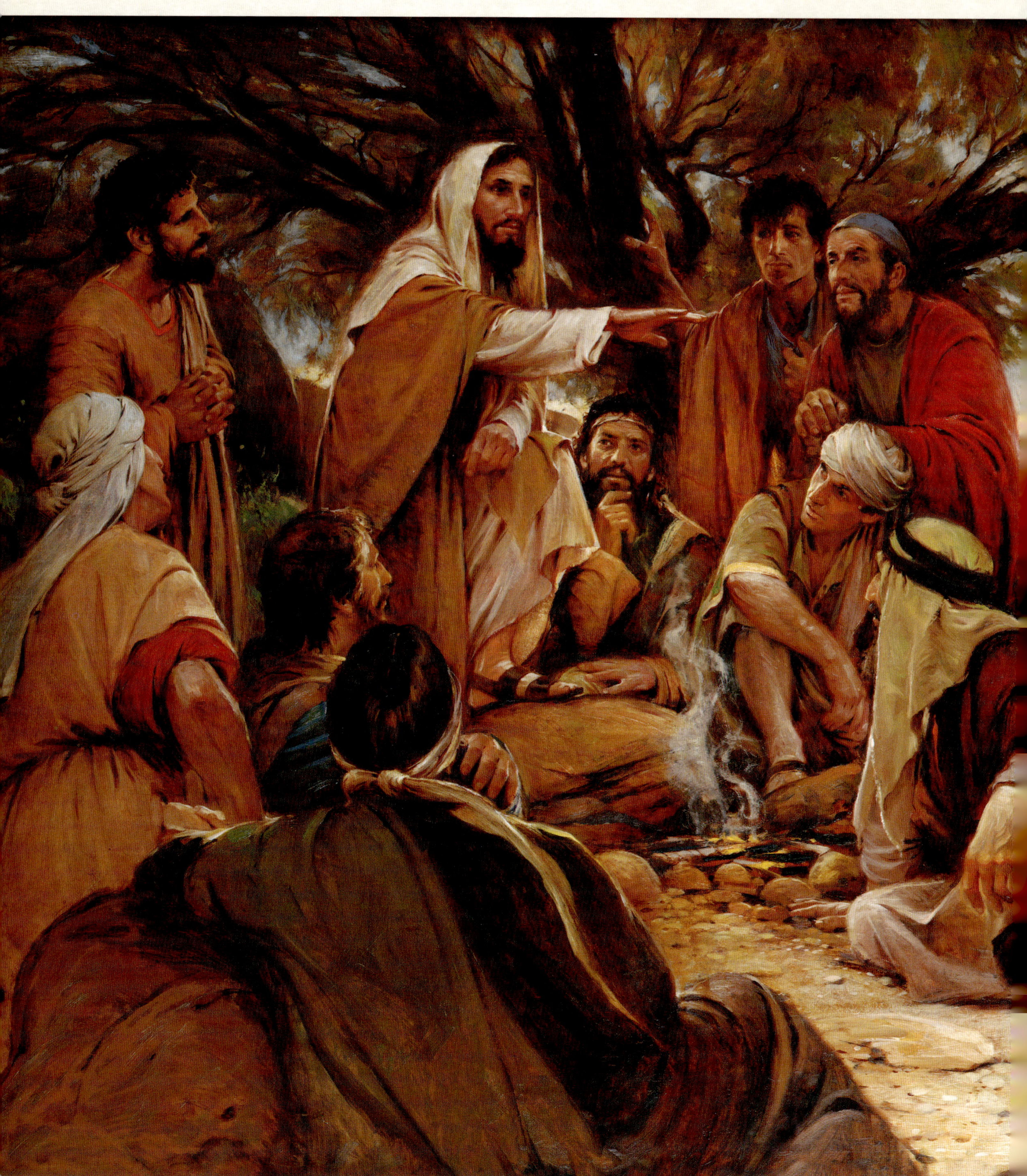

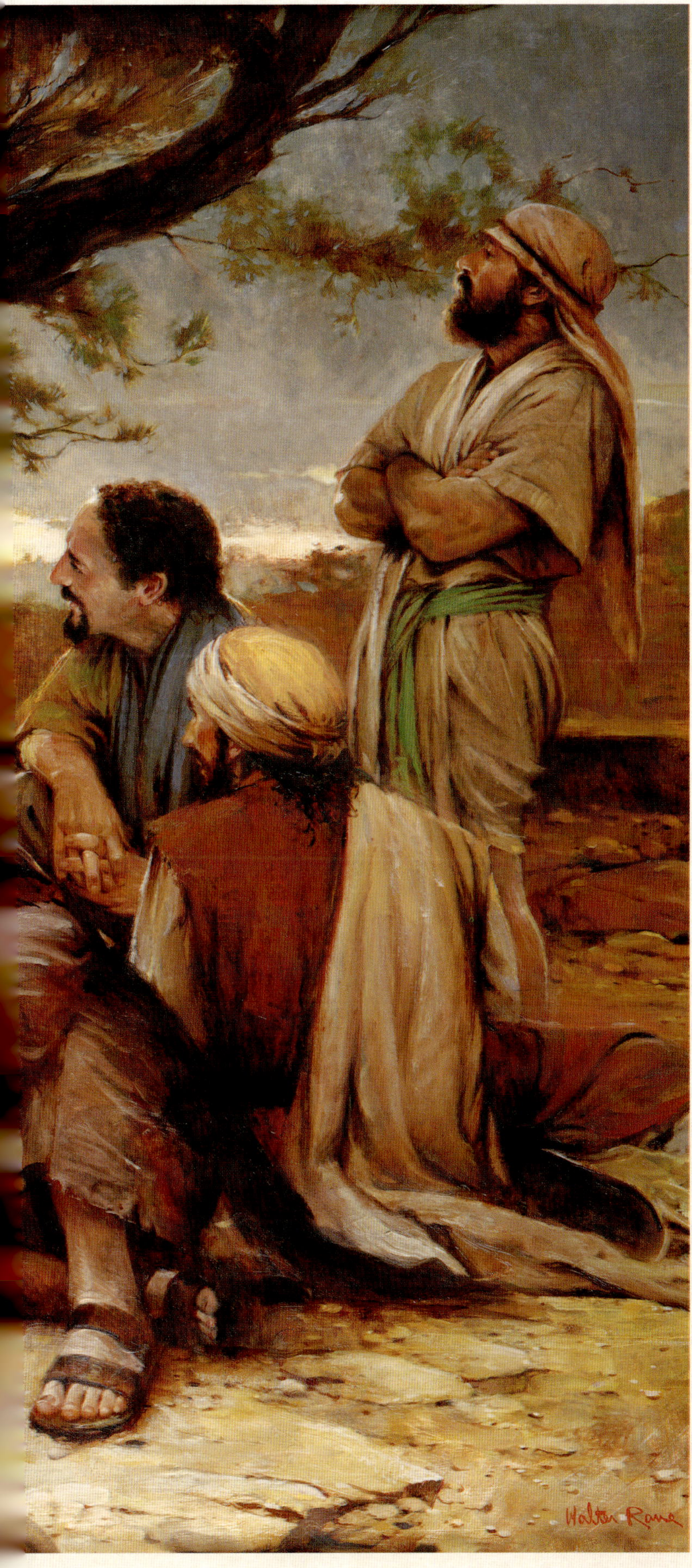

THE MOST IMPORTANT QUESTION IN human history is one which echoes down through the corridors of time; it will not go away: "Jesus asked them … what think ye of Christ?" (Matt. 22:41–42.) Sooner or later, this will be the vital question for all mortals, including you, my friends! A failure to answer this question *is* an answer.

Neal A. Maxwell, "Our Acceptance of Christ," *Ensign*, June 1984, 69

AND NOW, AFTER THE MANY TESTI-monies which have been given of him, this is the testimony, last of all, which we give of him: That he lives!

For we saw him, even on the right hand of God; and we heard the voice bearing record that he is the Only Begotten of the Father—

That by him, and through him, and of him, the worlds are and were created, and the inhabitants thereof are begotten sons and daughters unto God.

D&C 76:22-24

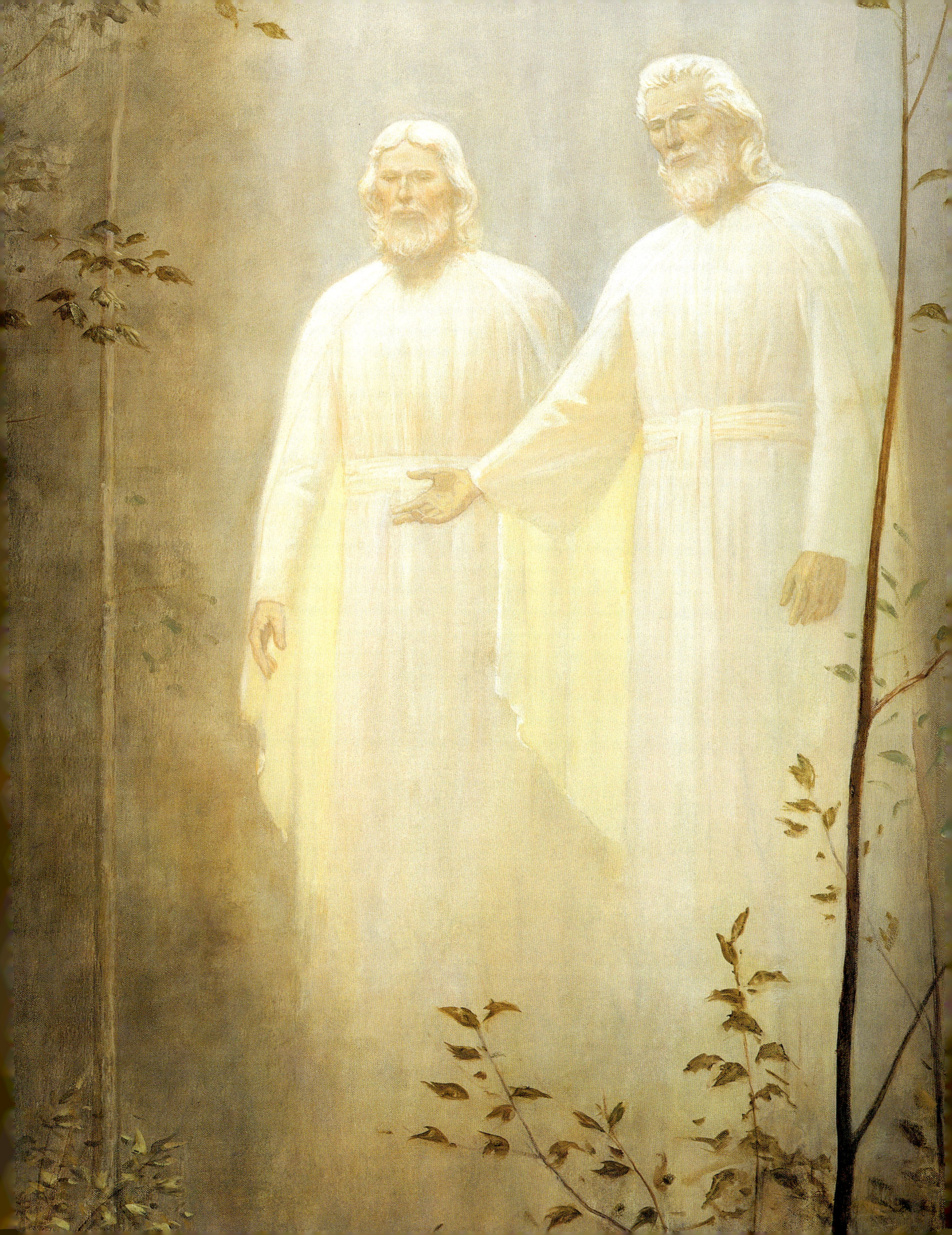

LIGHT OF THE WORLD

We bear testimony, as His duly ordained Apostles—that Jesus is **THE LIVING CHRIST,** *the immortal Son of God. He is the great King Immanuel, who stands today on the right hand of His Father. He is the light, the life, and the hope of the world. His way is the path that leads to happiness in this life and eternal life in the world to come. God be thanked for the matchless gift of His divine Son.*

The First Presidency and the Quorum of the Twelve, *The Living Christ: The Testimony of the Apostles*

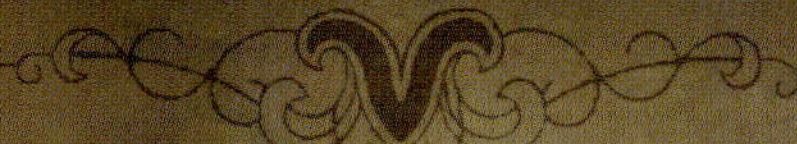

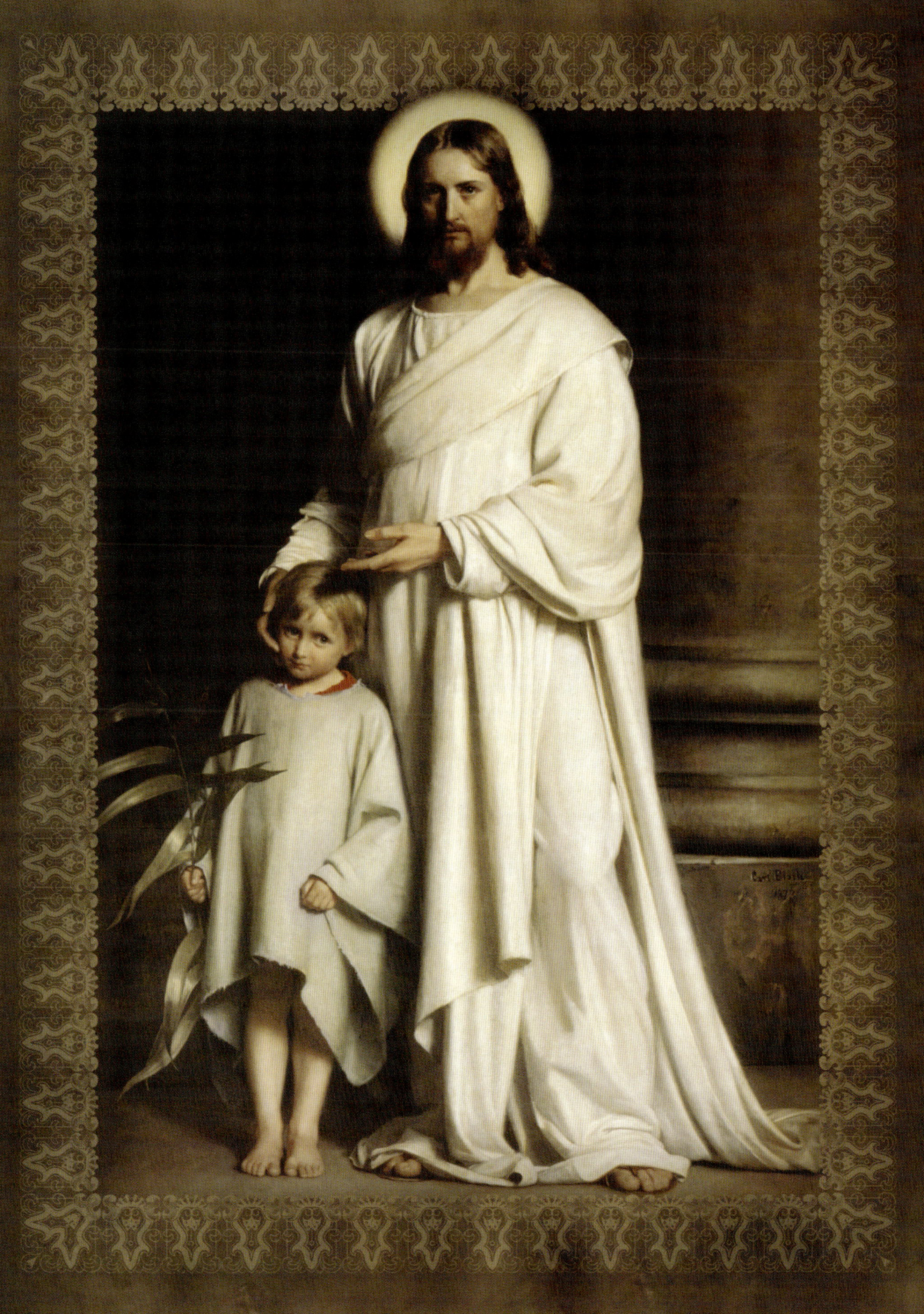

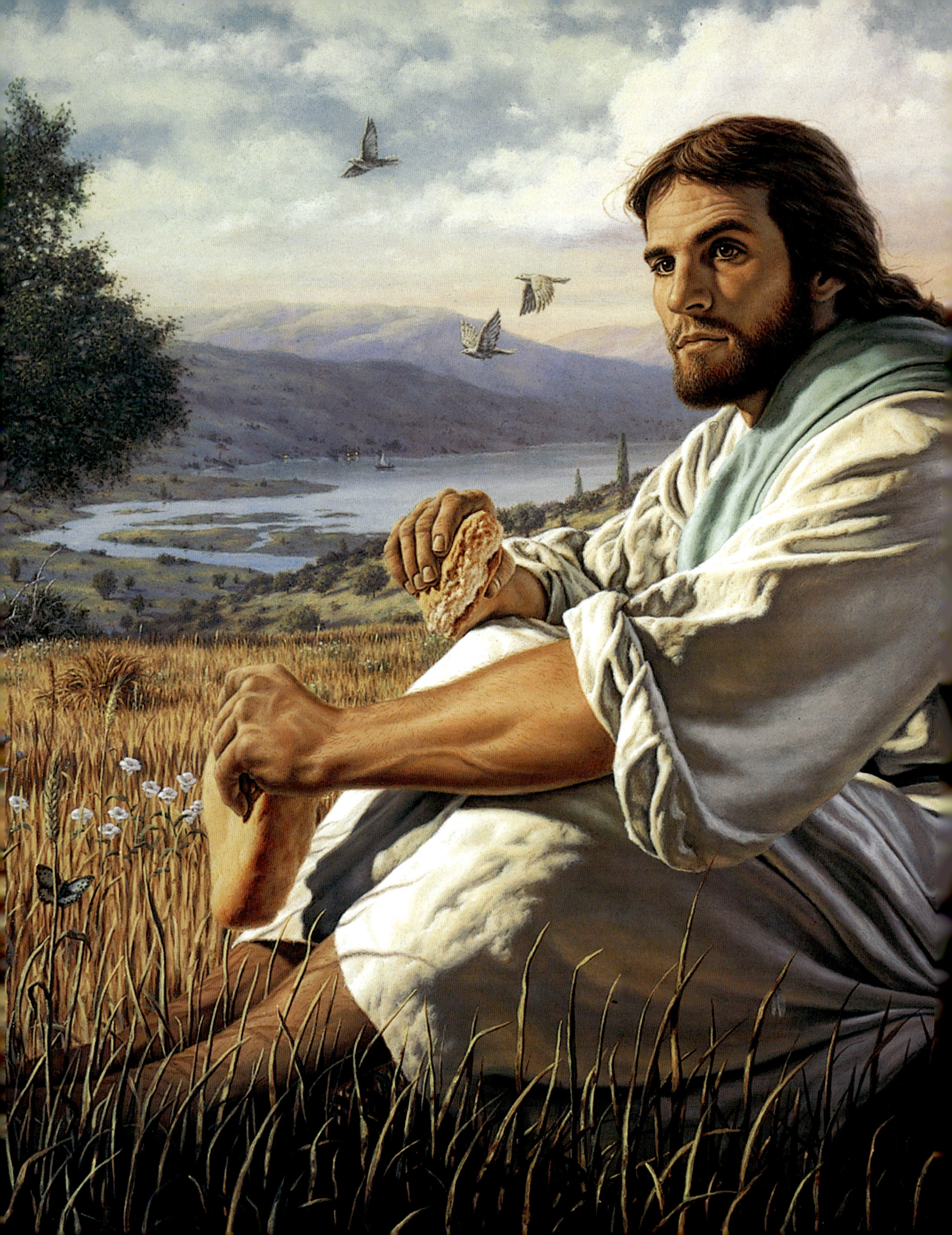

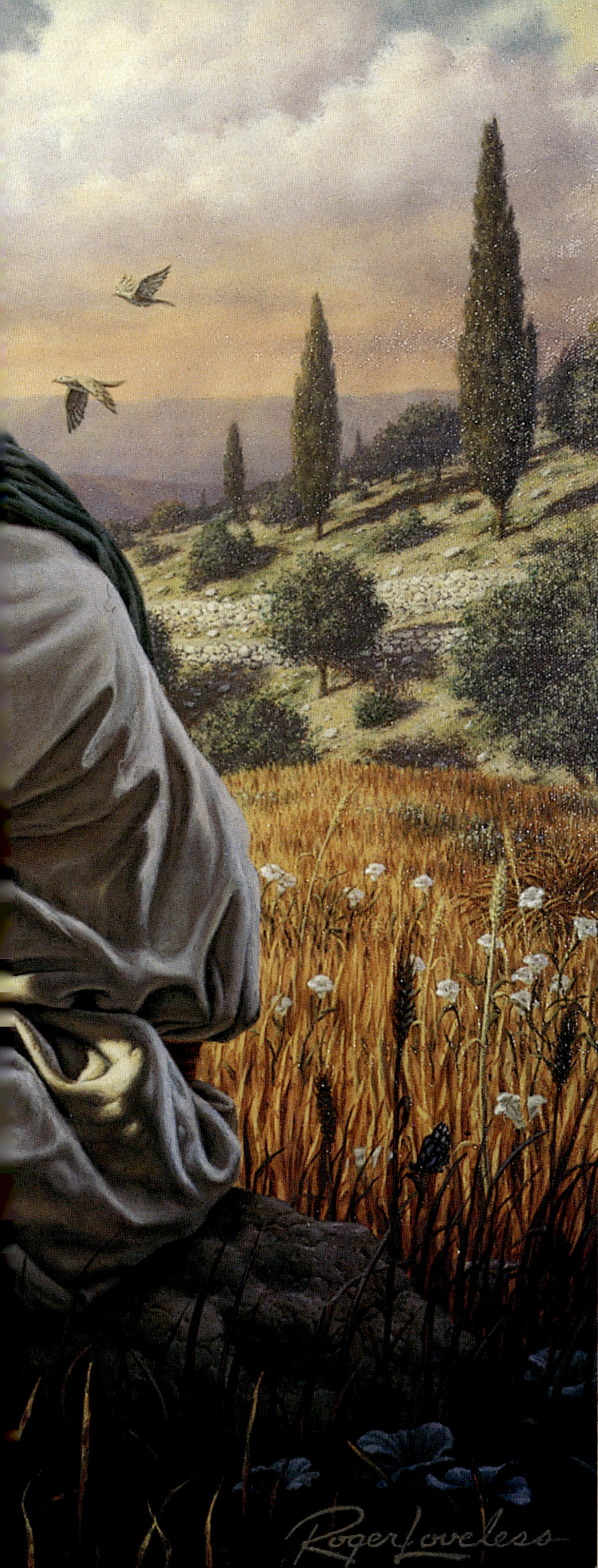

Then spake Jesus again unto them, saying,
I am the light of the world:
he that followeth me shall not walk in darkness,
but shall have the light of life.

John 8:12

MOST MEN YEARN FOR PEACE, CRY for peace, pray for peace, and work for peace, but there will not be lasting peace until all mankind follow the path pointed out and walked by the living Christ.

Marvin J. Ashton, "Peace—A Triumph of Principles," *Ensign*, November 1985, 69

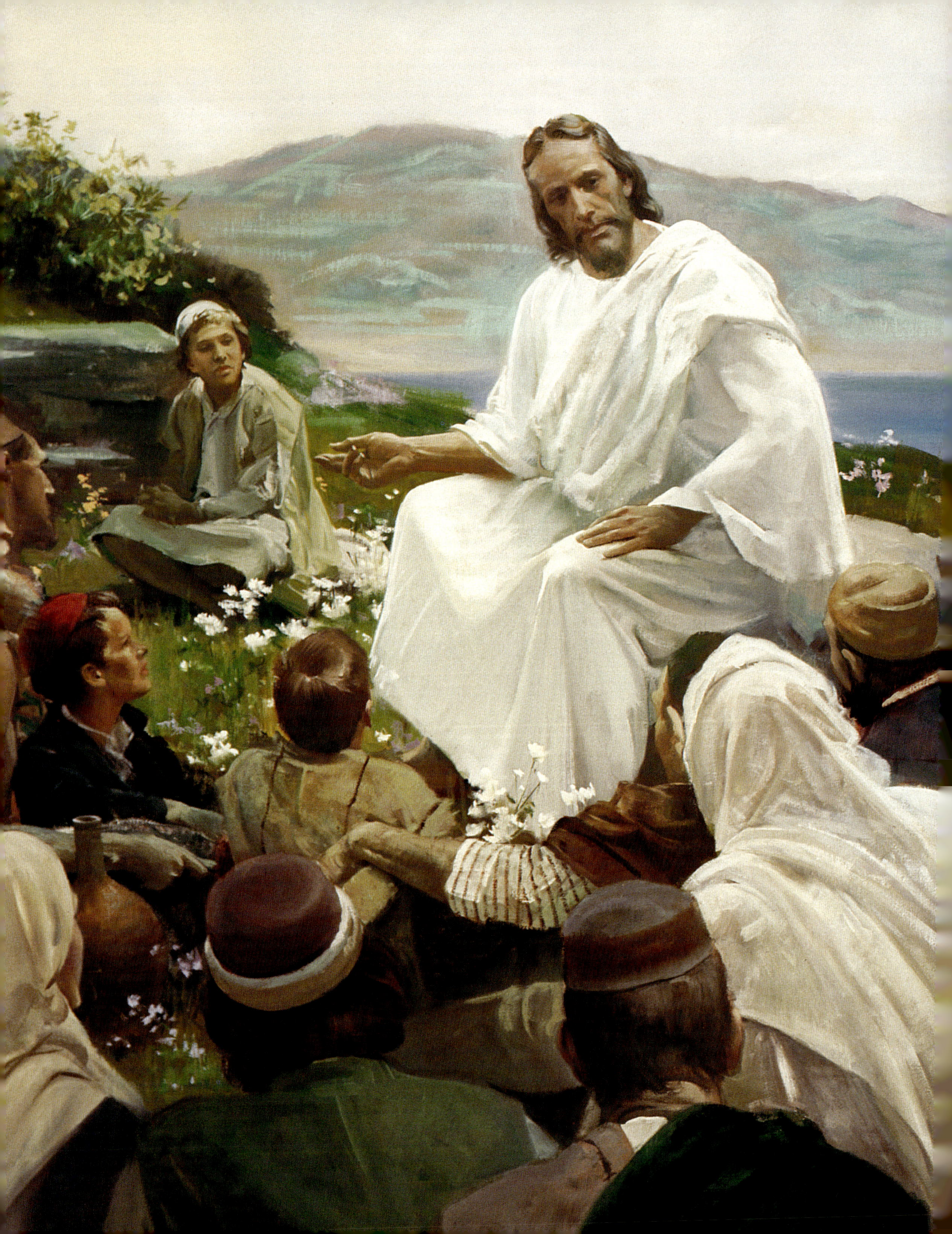

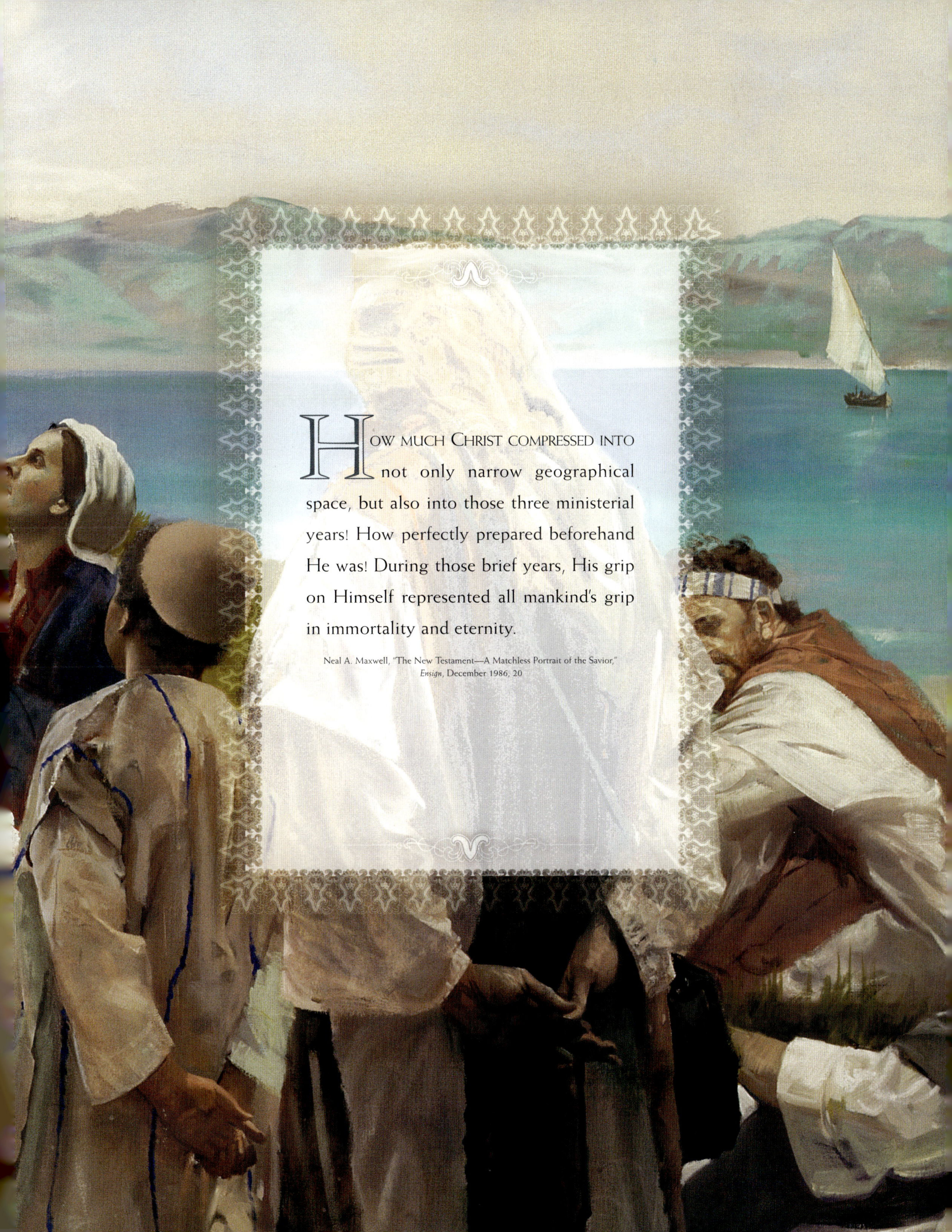

How much Christ compressed into not only narrow geographical space, but also into those three ministerial years! How perfectly prepared beforehand He was! During those brief years, His grip on Himself represented all mankind's grip in immortality and eternity.

Neal A. Maxwell, "The New Testament—A Matchless Portrait of the Savior," *Ensign*, December 1986, 20

JESUS CHRIST IS OUR REDEEMER AND Savior. He was begotten of the Father in the spirit, the Firstborn of the Father, and is the Only Begotten of the Father in the flesh. He is our elder brother. He is the second member of the Godhead. He was the Creator of heaven and earth under the direction of the Father. He is the Jehovah of the Old Testament. He is Jesus of Nazareth.

He is the Way, the Truth, and the Life. He is the Light of the world. He is the Author of our salvation. He was chosen before the foundation of the world to be the Lamb slain as an offering for our sins. Ultimately every knee must bow and every tongue confess that he is the Christ.

Joseph Andersen, "A Testimony of Christ," *Ensign*, November 1974, 101

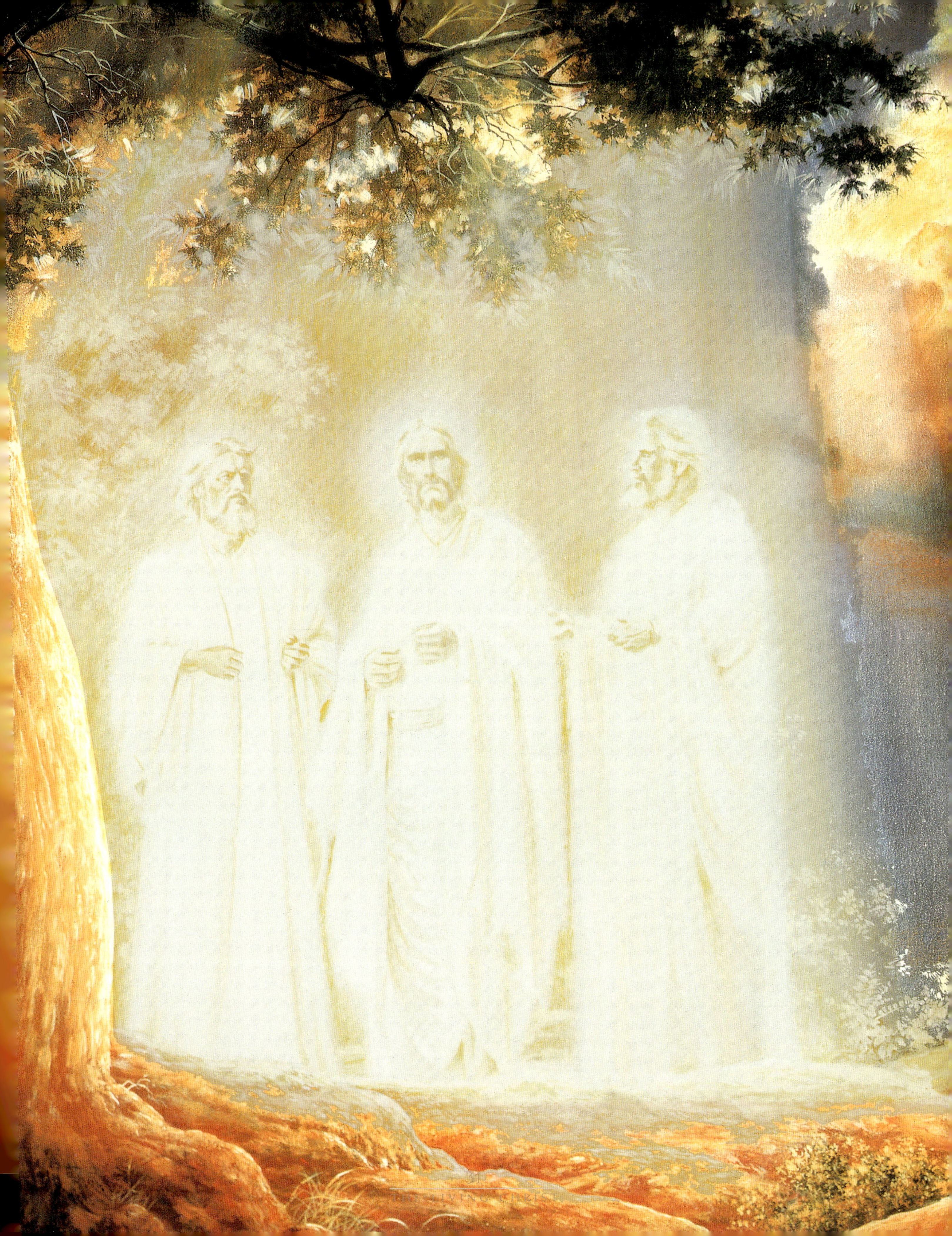

BEHOLD, I AM JESUS CHRIST THE SON of God. I created the heavens and the earth, and all things that in them are. I was with the Father from the beginning. I am in the Father, and the Father in me; and in me hath the Father glorified his name. . . .

I am the light and the life of the world. I am Alpha and Omega, the beginning and the end.

3 Nephi 9:13, 18

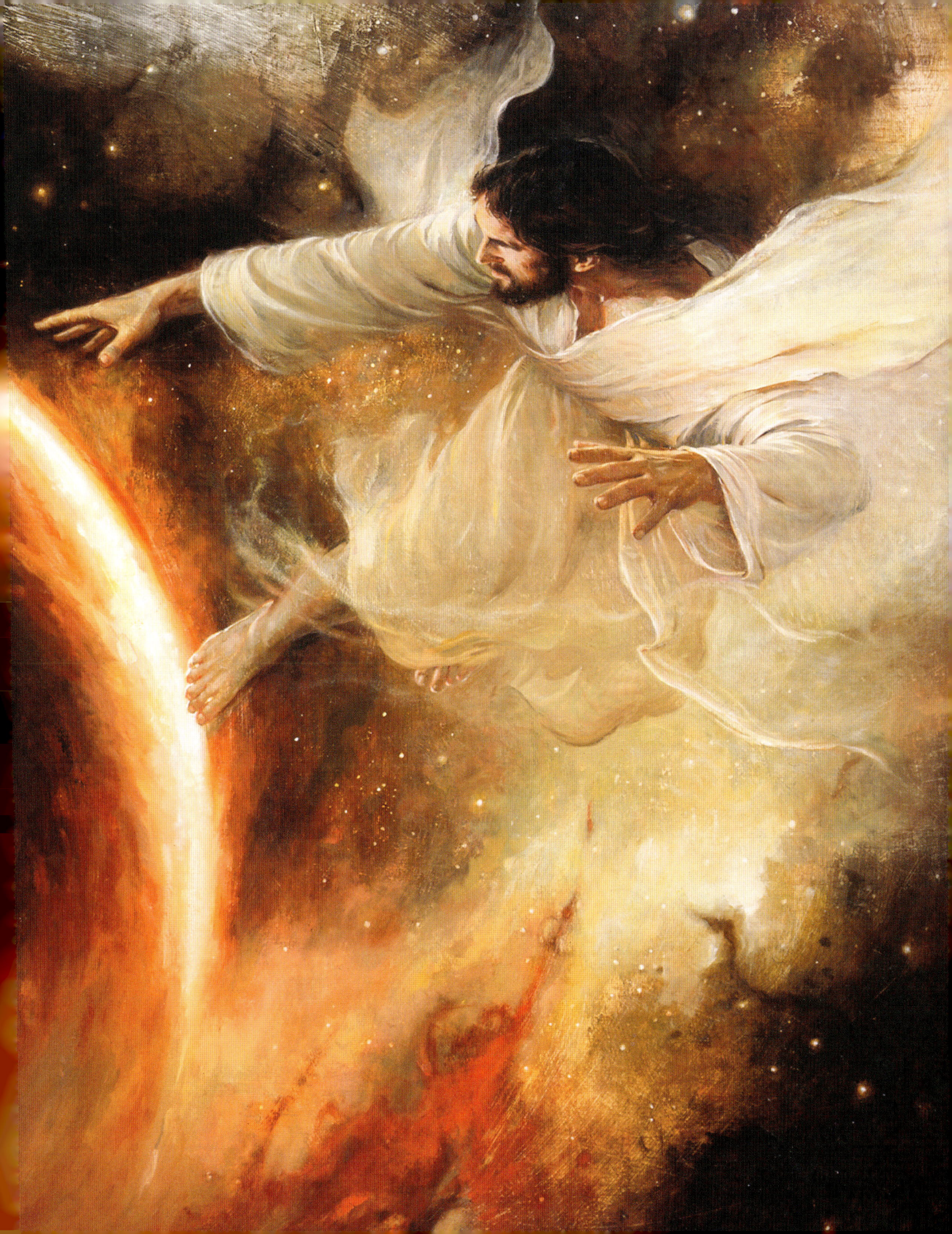

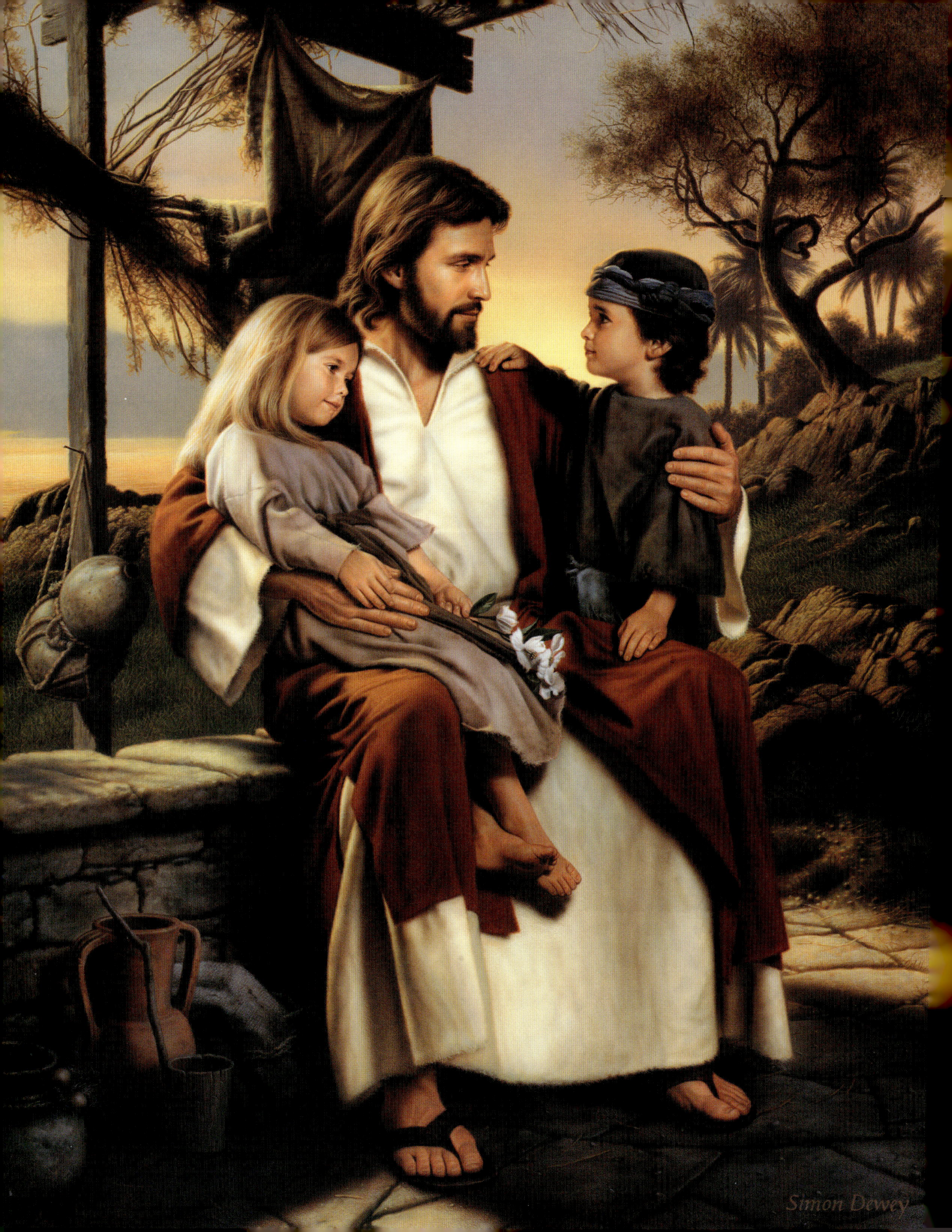
Simon Dewey

LET US REMEMBER THAT THE SAVIOR IS the Way, the Truth, and the Life, and there can be no greater promise than to know that if we are faithful and true, we will one day be safely encircled in the arms of His love (see D&C 6:20). He is always there to give encouragement, to forgive, and to rescue. Therefore, as we exercise faith and are diligent in keeping the commandments, we have nothing to fear from the journey.

M. Russell Ballard, "You Have Nothing to Fear From the Journey," *Ensign*, May 1977, 59

How do we accept Jesus of Nazareth?

We joyfully accept him without reservation as the greatest personage who ever lived on the face of the earth.

We believe him to be the Messiah, the Redeemer.

We glory in his mission and his doctrine.

We delight in him as the firstfruits of them that slept.

We worship him as the second member of the Godhead of three.

We humbly come to the Father through him, believing his words. "I am the way, the truth, and the life: no man cometh unto the Father, but by me." (John 14:6.)

James E. Faust, "The Resurrection," *Ensign*, May 1985, 30

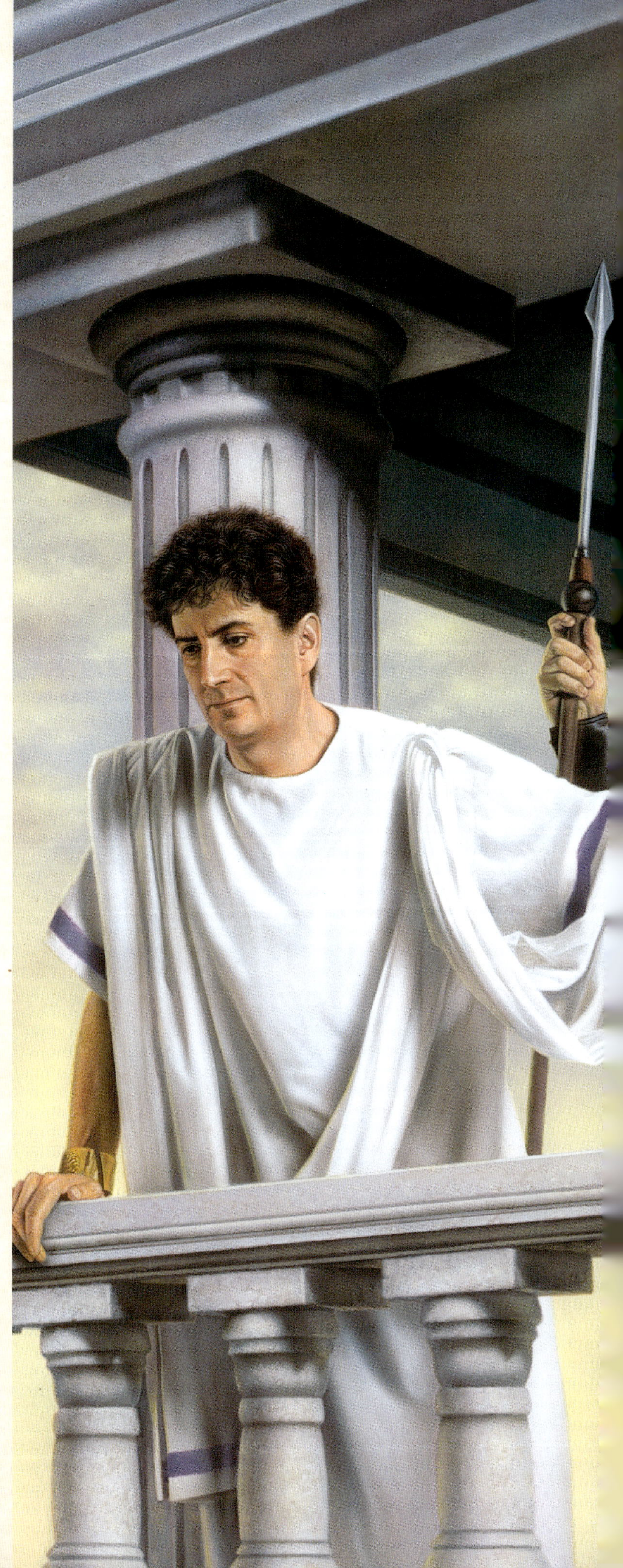

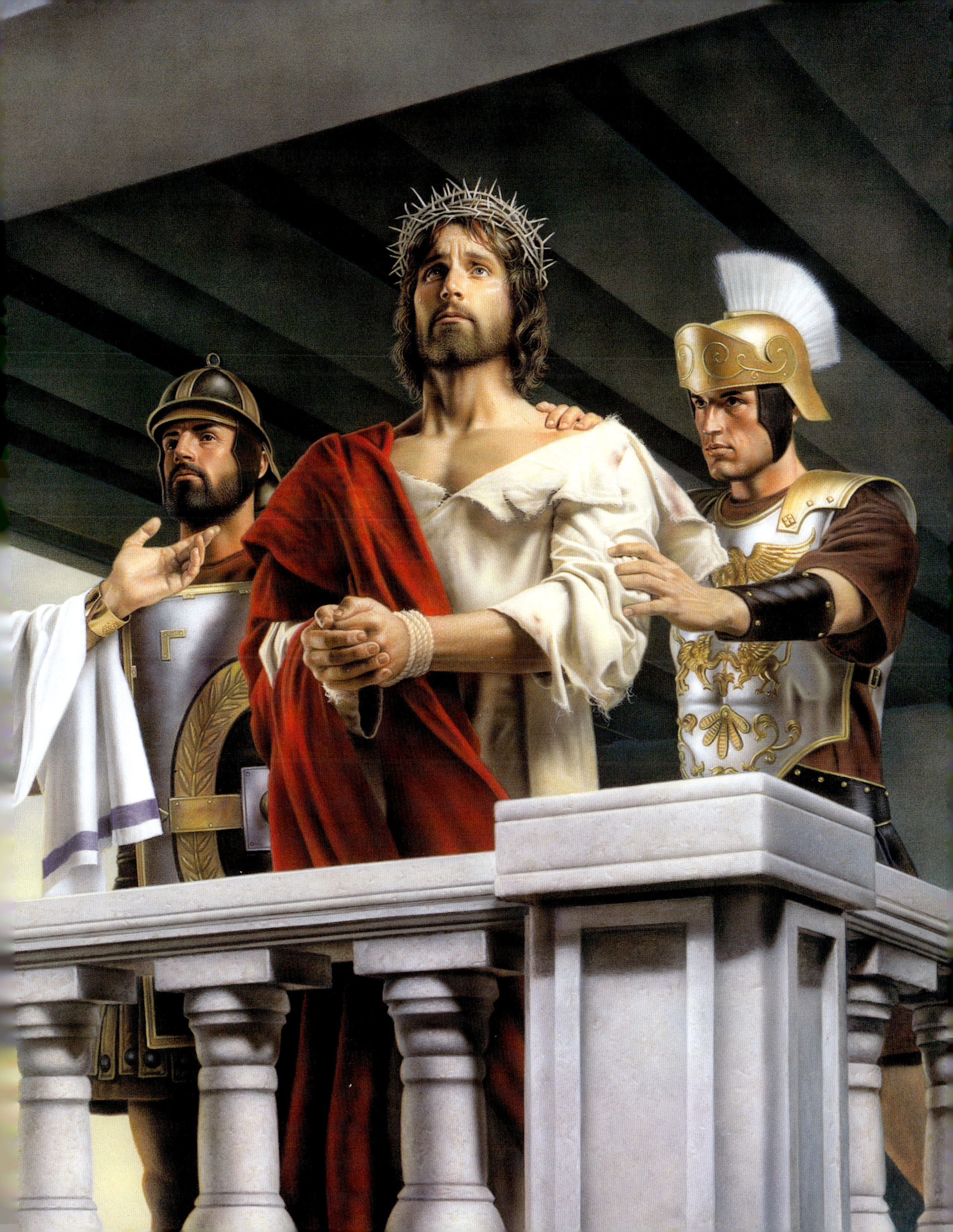

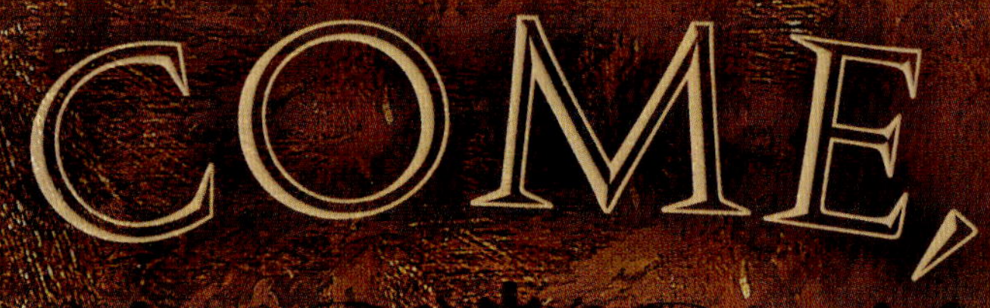

FOLLOW ME

It is my prayer that we will each live our lives and make our devotions in such a way as to be clearly recognizable . . . as true disciples of **THE LIVING CHRIST.** *But more important, I pray that we may be so recognized by the true and righteous Judge of us all, even the Lord Jesus Christ. What greater reward can any of us receive than to be acknowledged by Him as a true and faithful servant—a disciple, a friend.*

Richard C. Edgley, "A Disciple, a Friend," *Ensign*, May 1998, 11

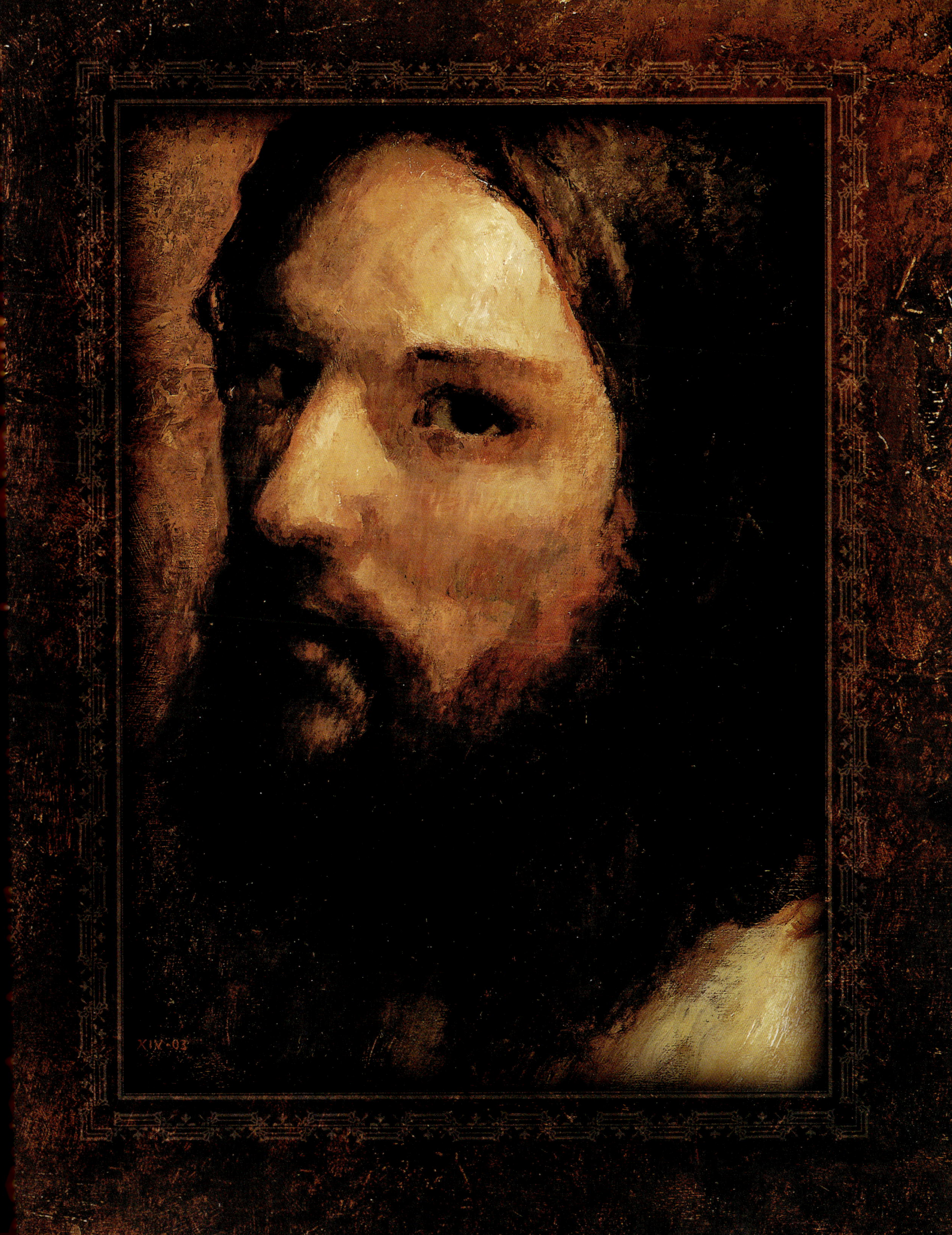
XIV·03

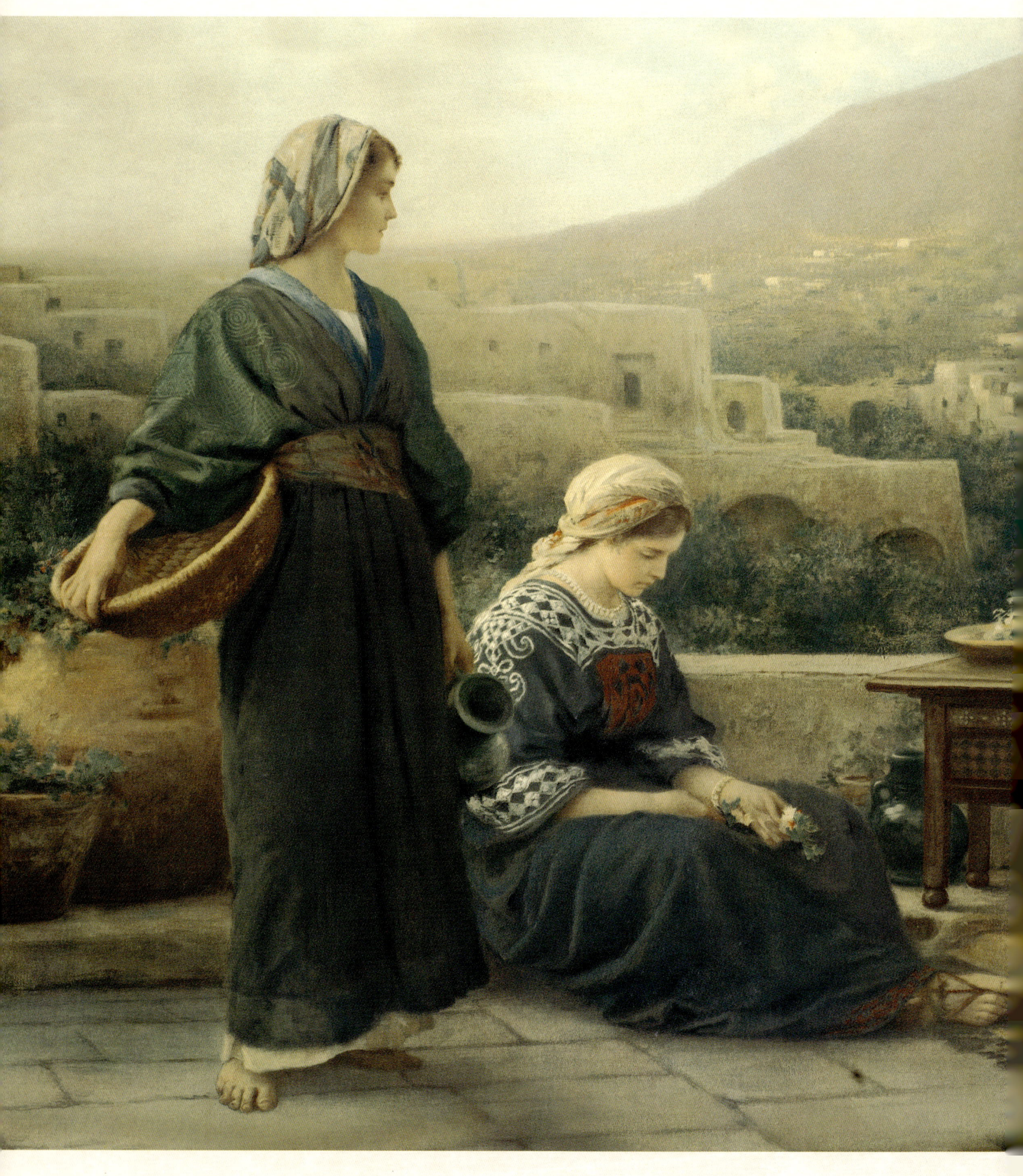

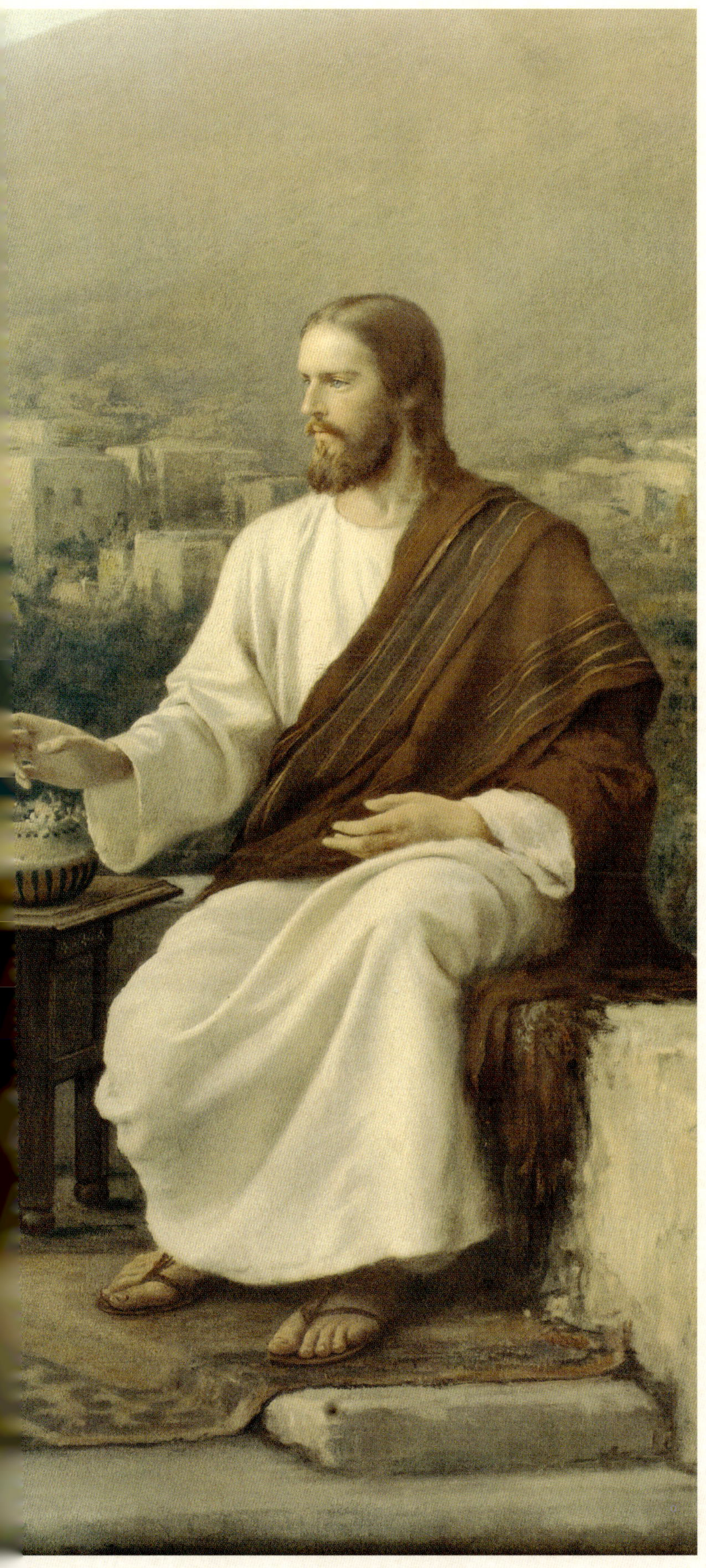

And again I say unto you, my friends, for from henceforth I shall call you friends . . . that ye become even as my friends in days when I was with them . . .

D&C 84:77

I testify that he is utterly incomparable in what he *is,* what he *knows,* what he has *accomplished,* and what he has *experienced.* Yet, movingly, he calls us his friends.

Neal A. Maxwell, "O, Divine Redeemer," *Ensign*, November 1981, 8

SINLESS AND FLAWLESS AS JESUS WAS IN mortality, we should remember that He viewed His own state of physical perfection as being yet in the future. Even He had to endure to the end. Can you and I be expected to do less?

Russell M. Nelson, "Jesus the Christ: Our Master and More," *Ensign*, April 2000, 5

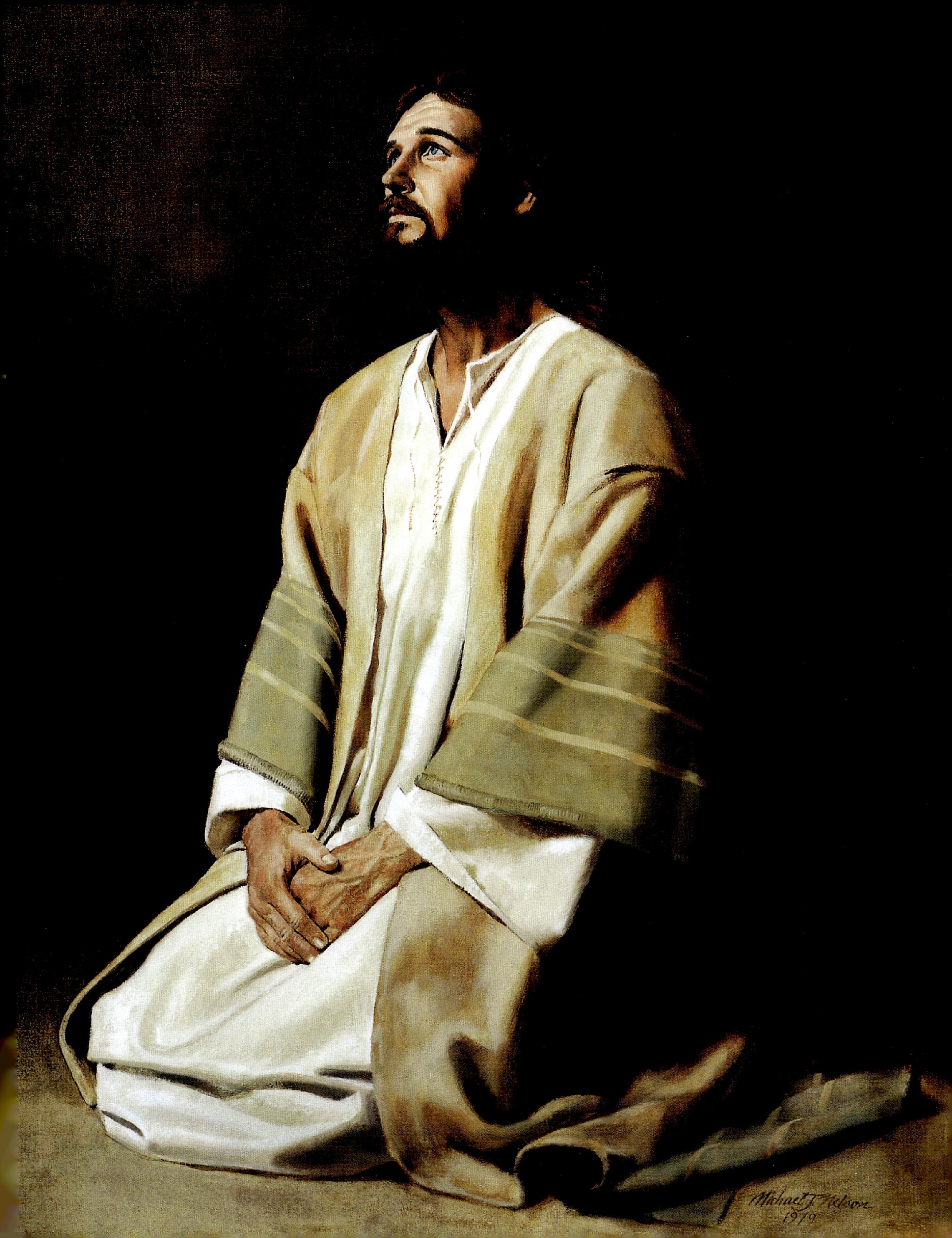
Michael T. Nelson
1979

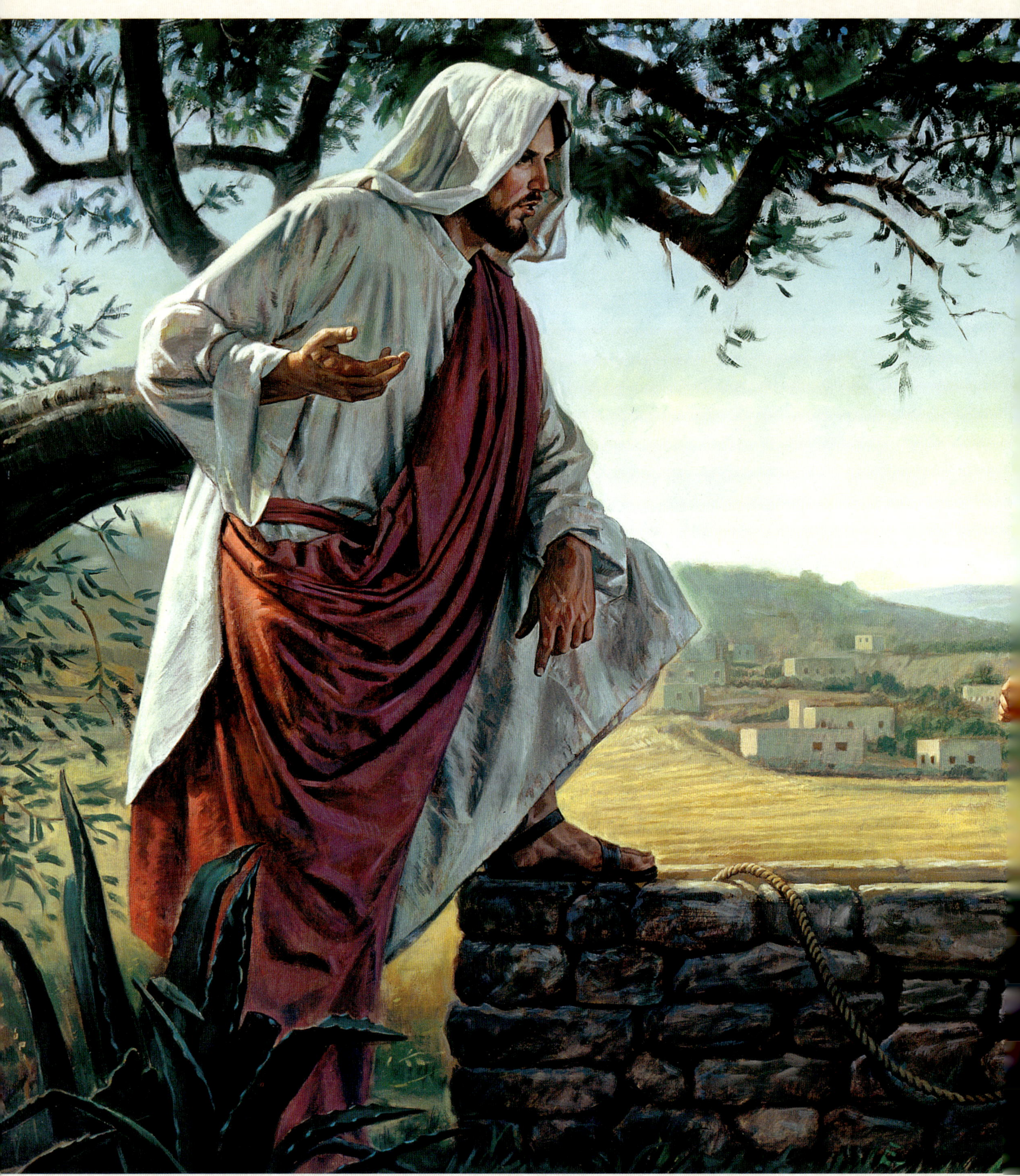

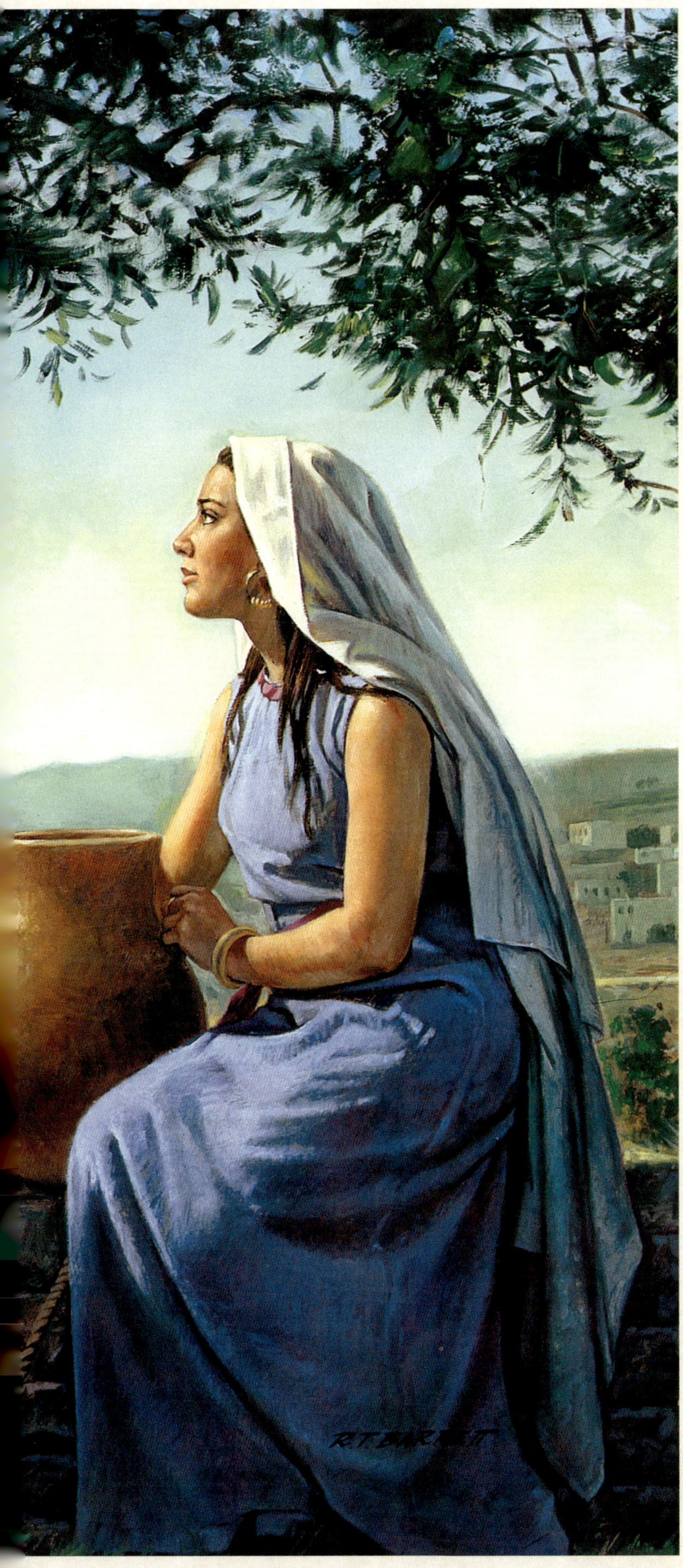

WE CANNOT REALLY LEARN ANY deep or lasting things about Jesus unless we take His yoke upon us. Then, though on our small scales compared to His, the relevant experiences will teach us keenly and deeply about Him and His divine attributes. There is nothing abstract about it at all. It becomes a very personal thing for us.

Neal A. Maxwell, "Jesus, the Perfect Mentor," *Ensign*, February 2001, 8

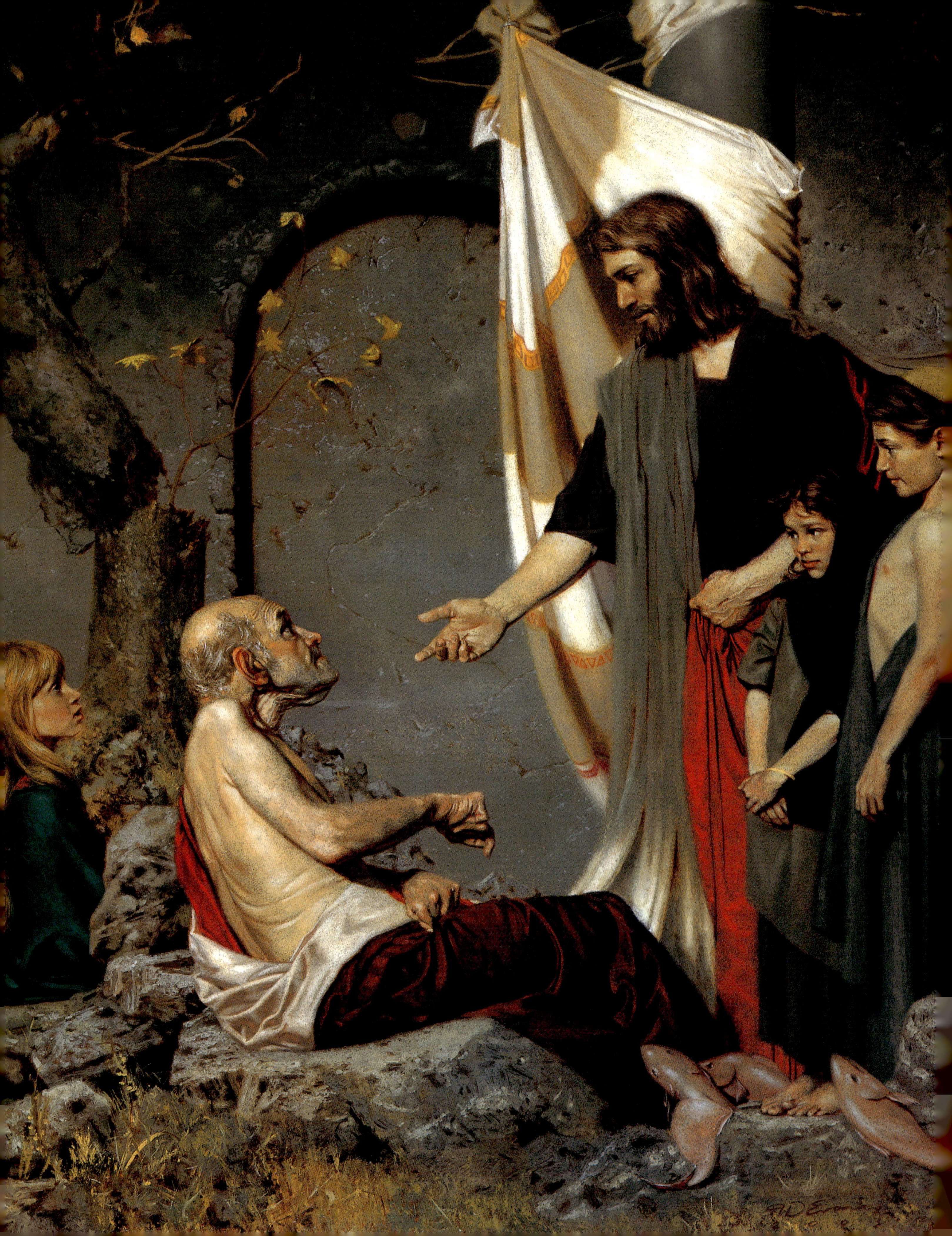

Come unto me, all ye that labour and are heavy laden, and I will give you rest.

Take my yoke upon you, and learn of me; for I am meek and lowly in heart: and ye shall find rest unto your souls.

Matthew 11:28–29

IN THE CHOICES WE MAKE IN LIFE, WE need to know the Savior. His simple admonition *"Come . . . follow me"* could transform human existence if we would let it. He has the power to make our burdens light if we will turn to Him.

Robert D. Hales, "Special Witnesses of Christ," *Ensign*, April 2001, 4

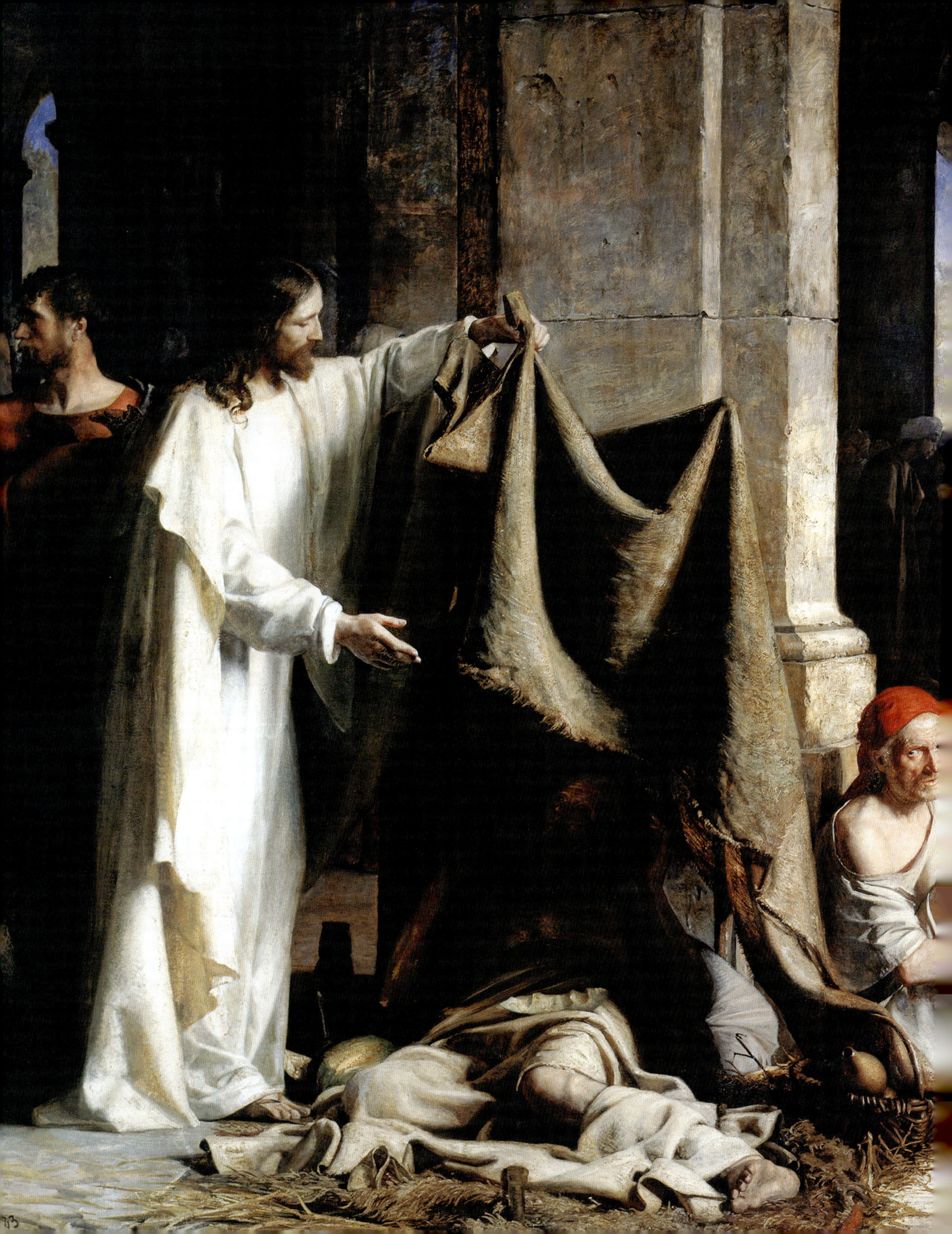

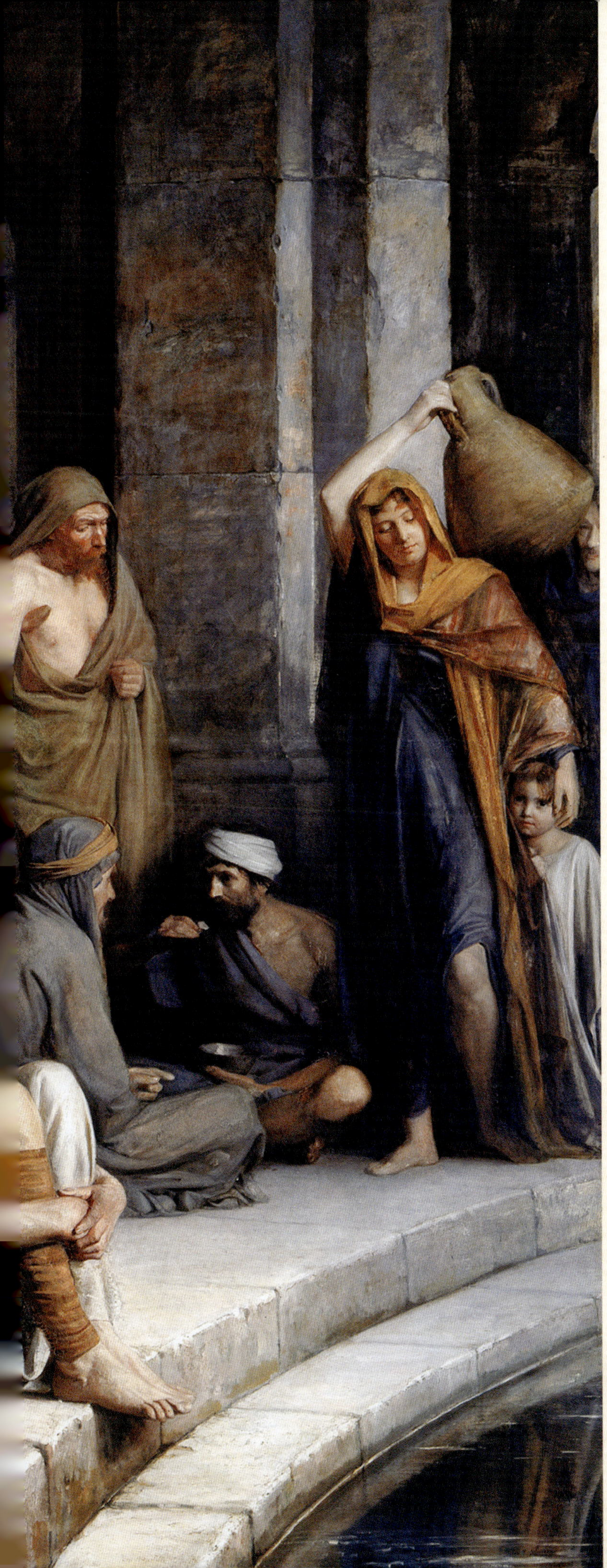

THE LORD WORKS FROM THE INSIDE OUT. The world works from the outside in. The world would take people out of the slums. Christ takes the slums out of the people, and then they take themselves out of the slums. . . . Christ changes men, who then change their environment. The world would shape human behavior, but Christ can change human nature.

Ezra Taft Benson, "Born of God," *Ensign*, July 1989, 2

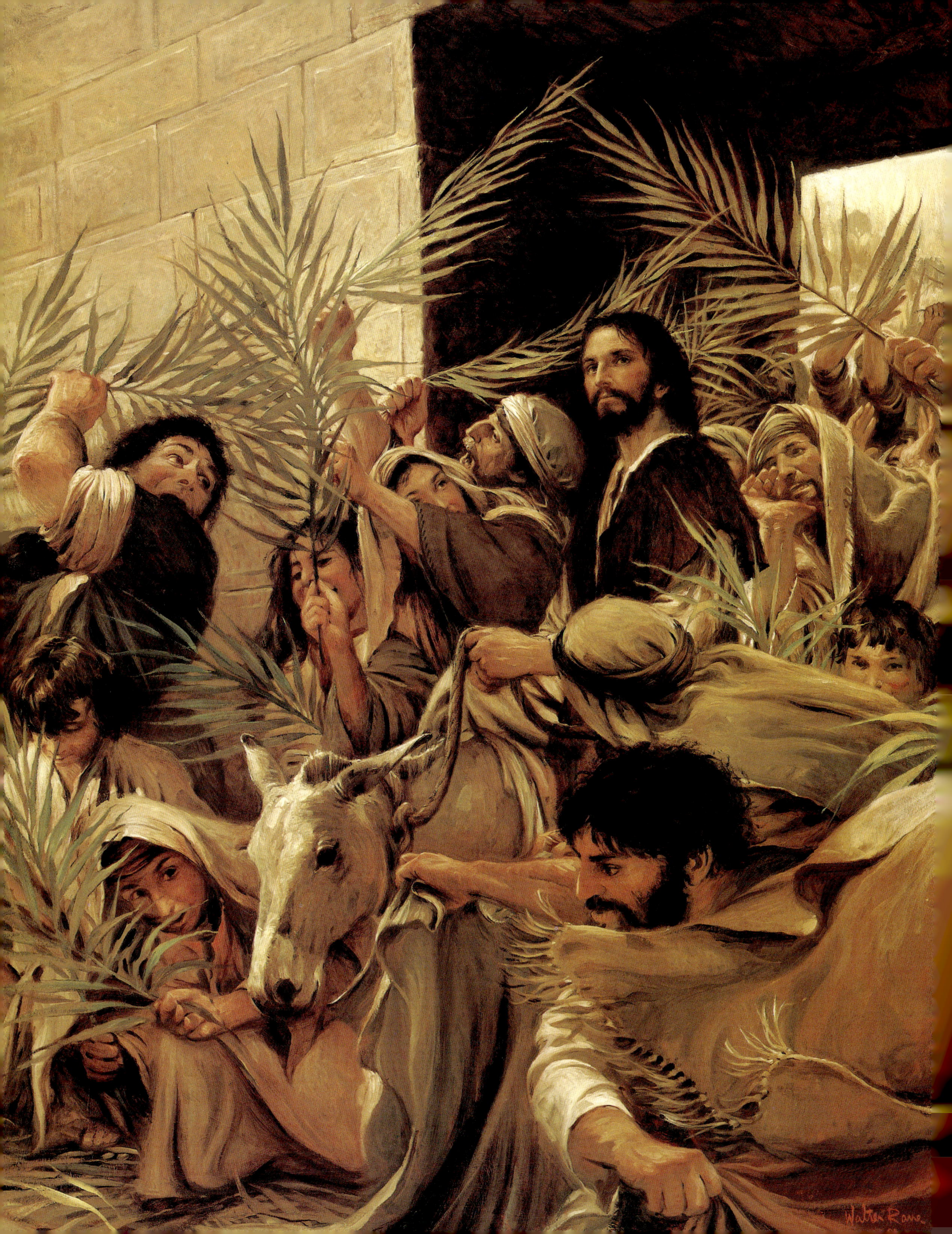

IF WE TRULY UNDERSTAND THE FULL STATURE of the name by which we are called, we will live different lives. No longer will we do less than our best in our work or at school. No longer will we be dishonest in paying our bills or in the treatment of our family members, nor will we take unfair advantage of anyone in *any* way. Our word will be as binding on us as our bond. No longer will we be unkind to our associates or be unvirtuous or immoral or selfish in any way, either secretly or openly. We will do nothing to bring dishonor or shame to that holy name we carry as children of Jesus Christ. We will respect and honor our covenant Father, Jesus Christ, and be righteously jealous and protective of the holy name we bear. We will judge everything we do on the basis of how it might reflect on Him whose name we carry, not only on our lips but in our very hearts.

Theodore M. Burton, "To Be Born Again," *Ensign*, September 1985, 66

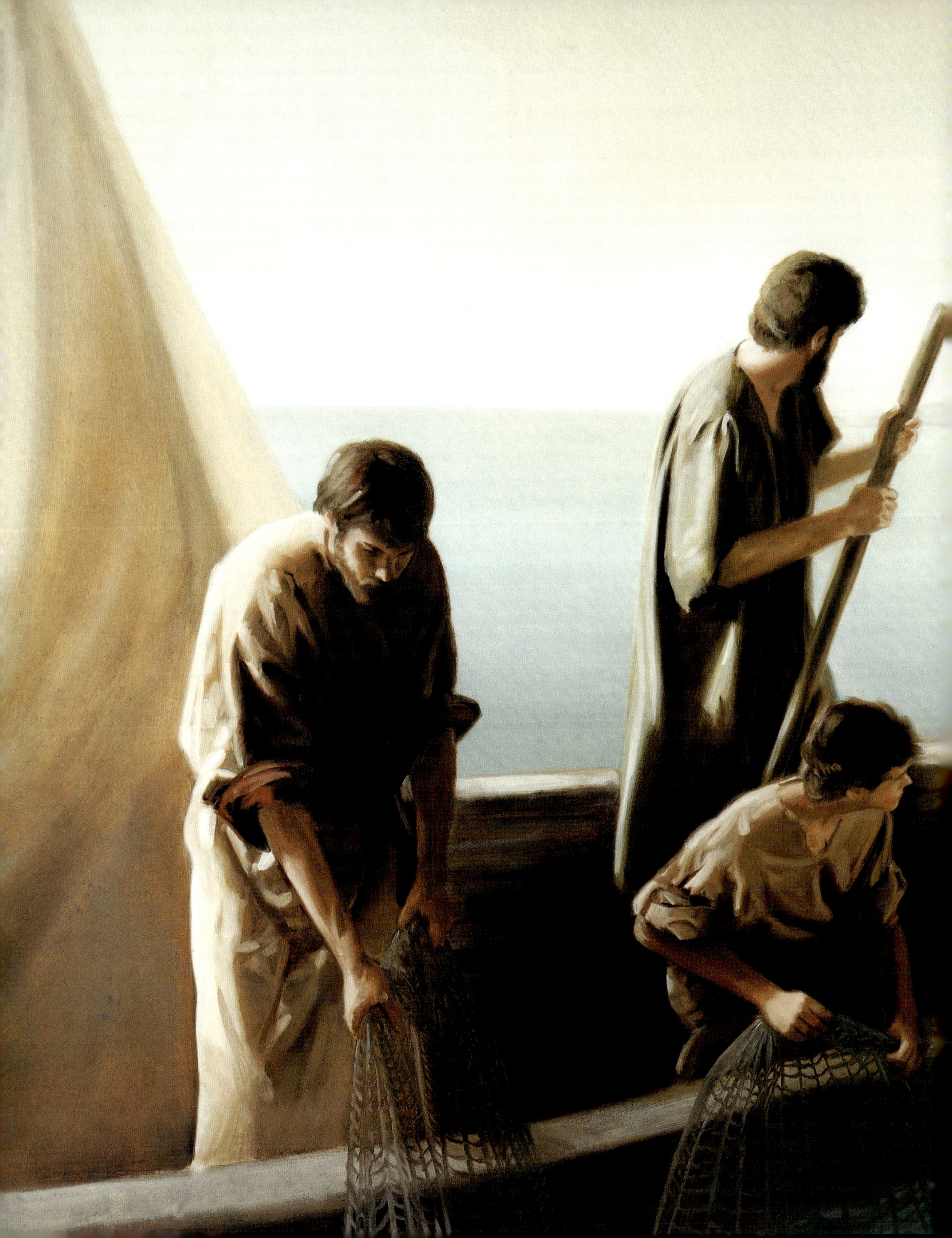

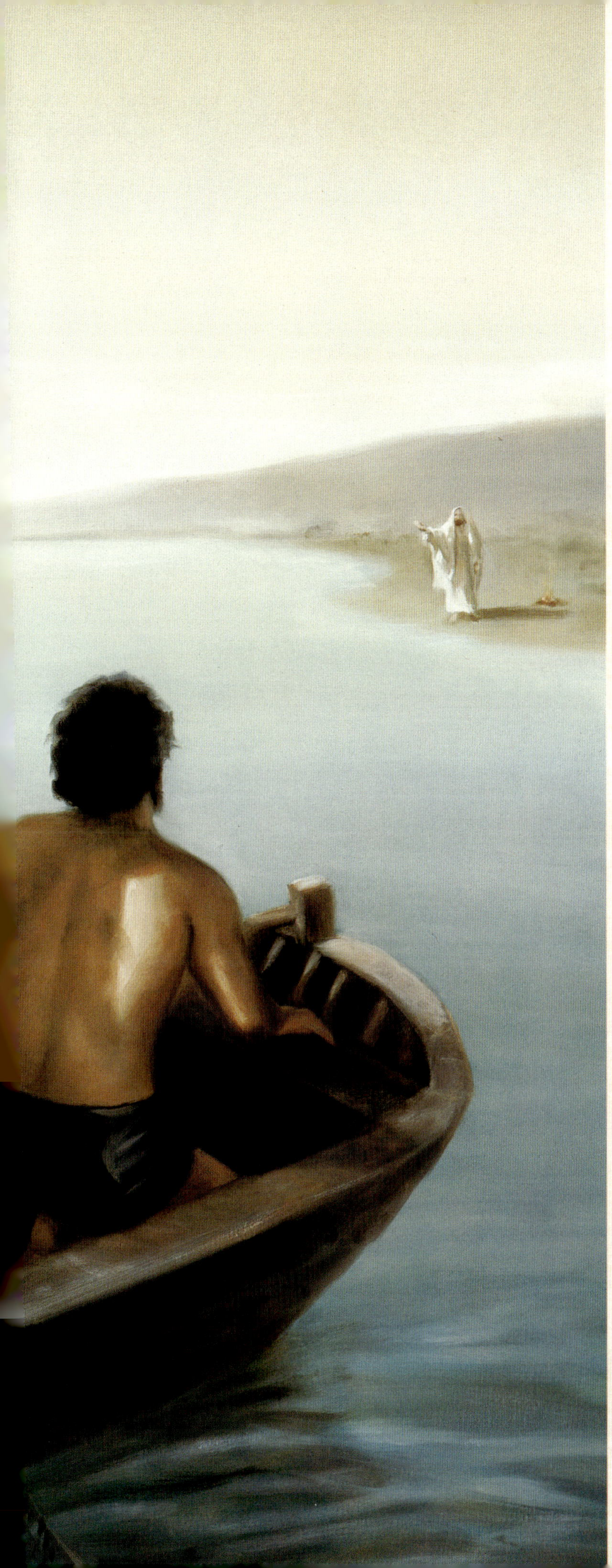

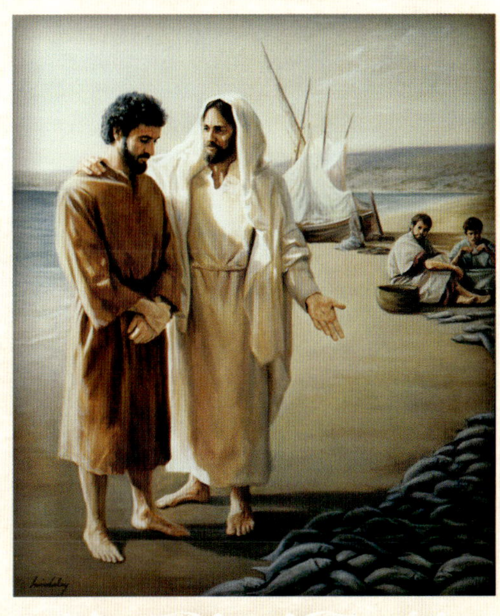

CHRIST SAYS, "GIVE ME ALL. I DON'T want so much of your time and so much of your money and so much of your work: I want You. I have not come to torment your natural self, but to kill it. No half-measures are any good. I don't want to cut off a branch here and a branch there, I want to have the whole tree down. . . . Hand over the whole natural self, all the desires which you think innocent as well as the ones you think wicked—the whole outfit. I will give you a new self instead. In fact, I will give you Myself: my own will shall become yours."

C.S. Lewis, *Mere Christianity* (New York: Collier Books, 1960), 167

One of the great teachings of the Man of Galilee, the Lord Jesus Christ, was that you and I carry within us immense possibilities. In urging us to be perfect as our Father in Heaven is perfect, Jesus was not taunting us or teasing us. He was telling us a powerful truth about our possibilities and about our potential. It is a truth almost too stunning to contemplate. Jesus, who could not lie, sought to beckon us to move further along the pathway to perfection.

Spencer W. Kimball, "Jesus: The Perfect Leader," *Ensign,* August 1979, 5

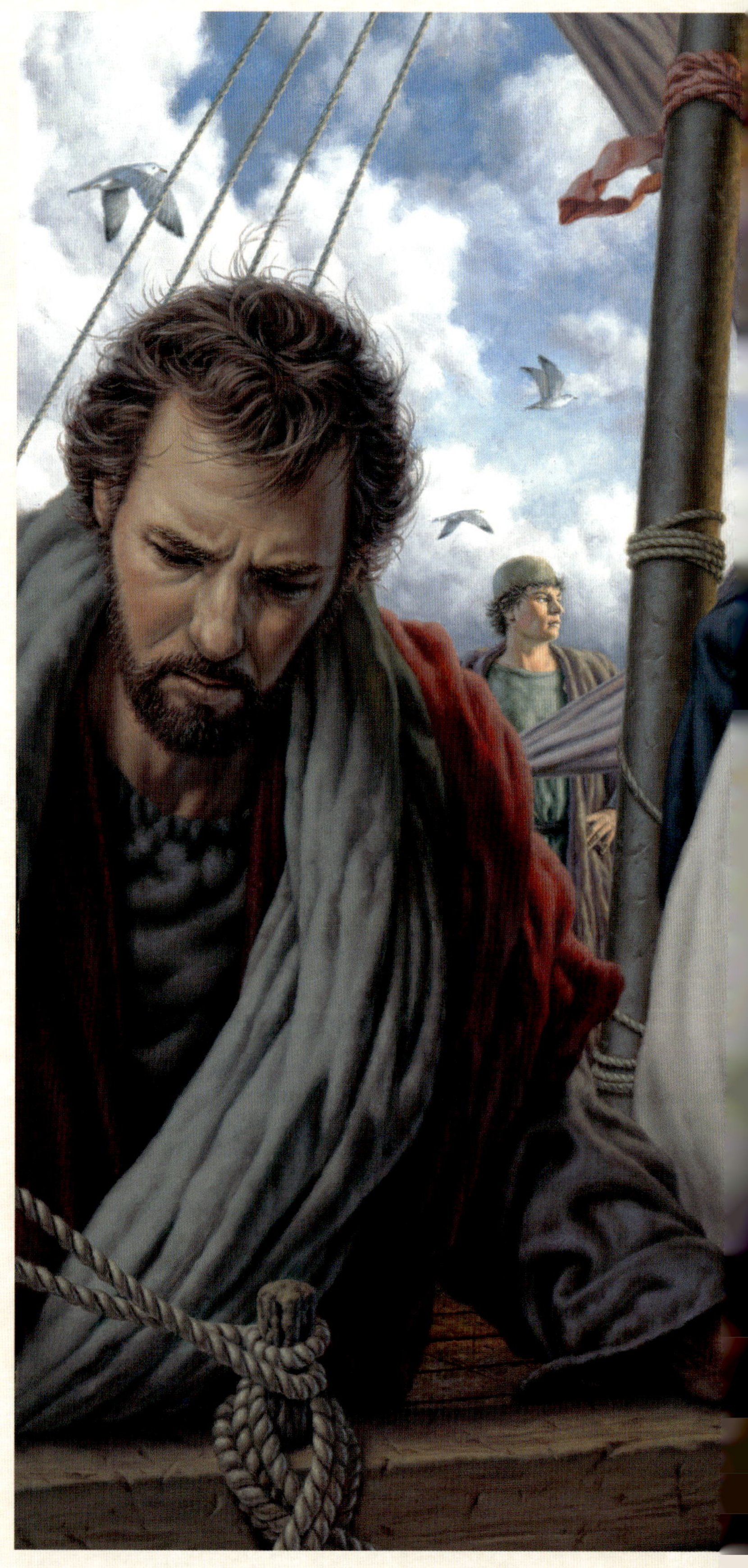

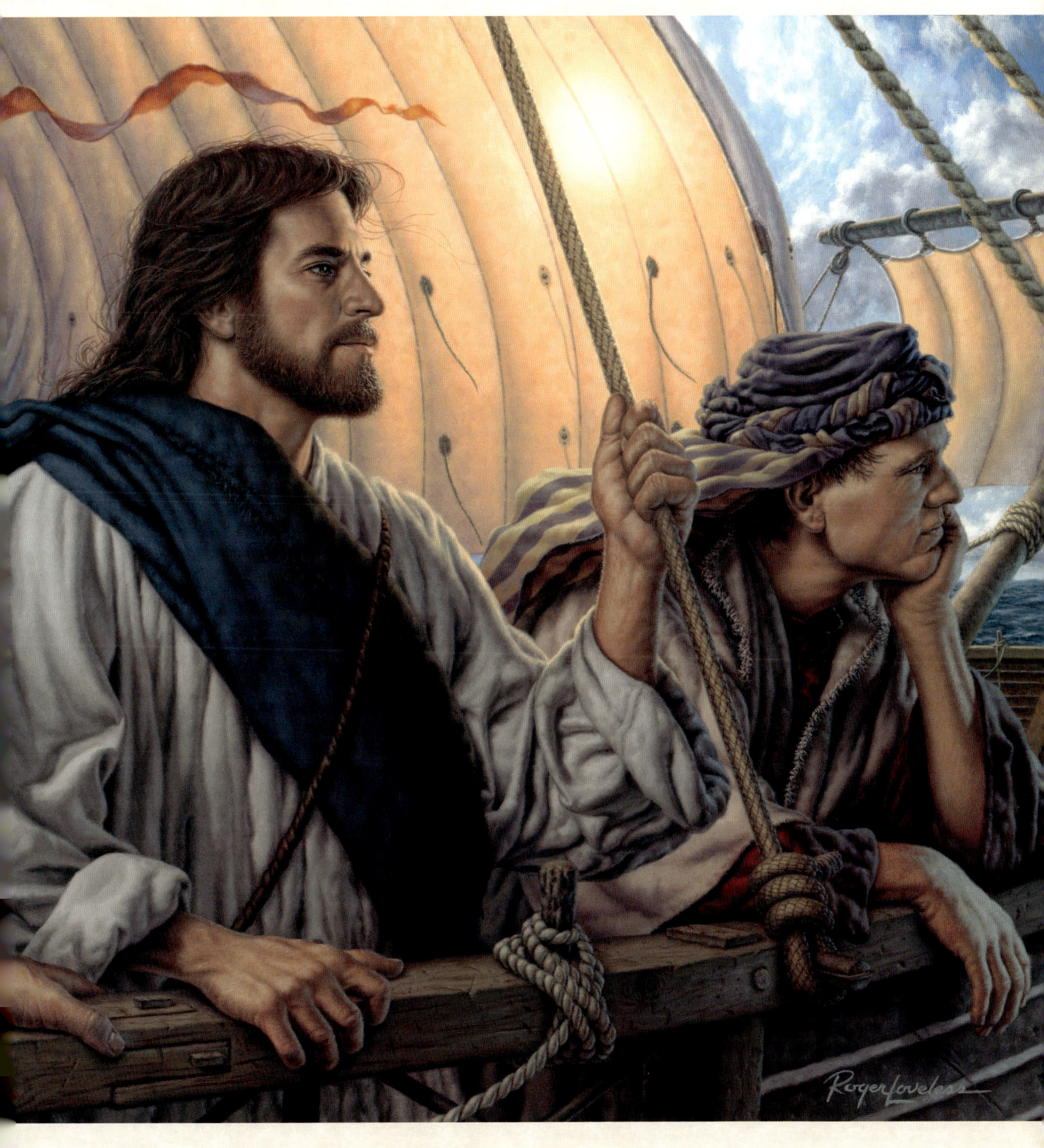
Roger Loveless

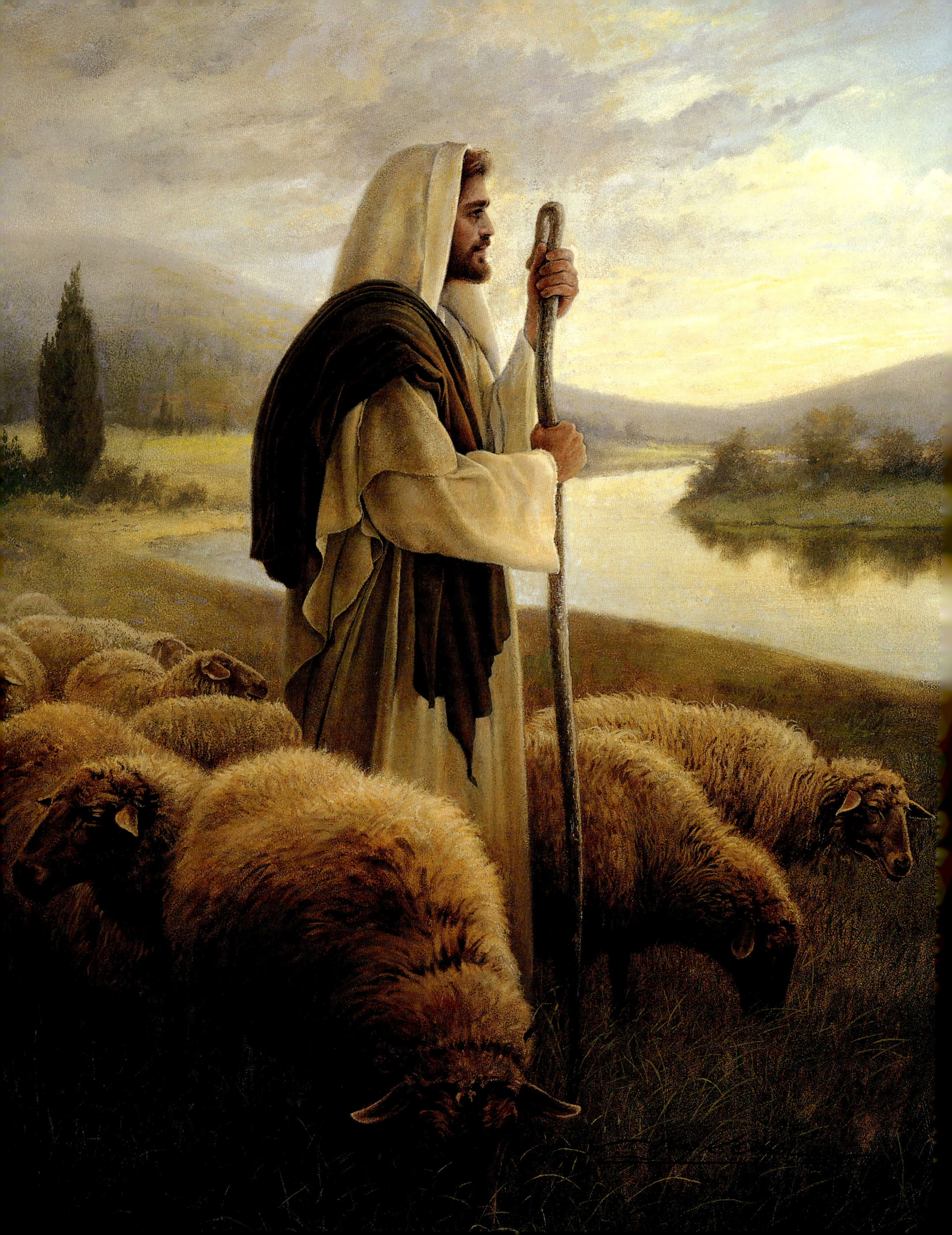

I am the good shepherd,

and know my sheep,

and am known of mine.

John 10:14

OUR HEAVENLY FATHER WOULD NOT be the Perfect Father, nor Jesus our Perfect Shepherd, if they were content with us as we now are. Why? Because they know what we have the power to become!

Neal A. Maxwell, "The New Testament—A Matchless Portrait of the Savior," *Ensign*, December 1986, 20

HIS ATONING SACRIFICE

We rejoice in the knowledge of THE LIVING CHRIST, *and we reverently acknowledge the miracles He continues to work today in the lives of those who have faith in Him. He is the head of the Church, which bears His name. He is our Savior and our Redeemer. Through Him we worship and pray to our Heavenly Father. We are grateful beyond measure for the essential and awesome power His Atonement has in each of our lives.*

M. Russell Ballard, "How Is It with Us?" *Ensign*, May 2000, 31

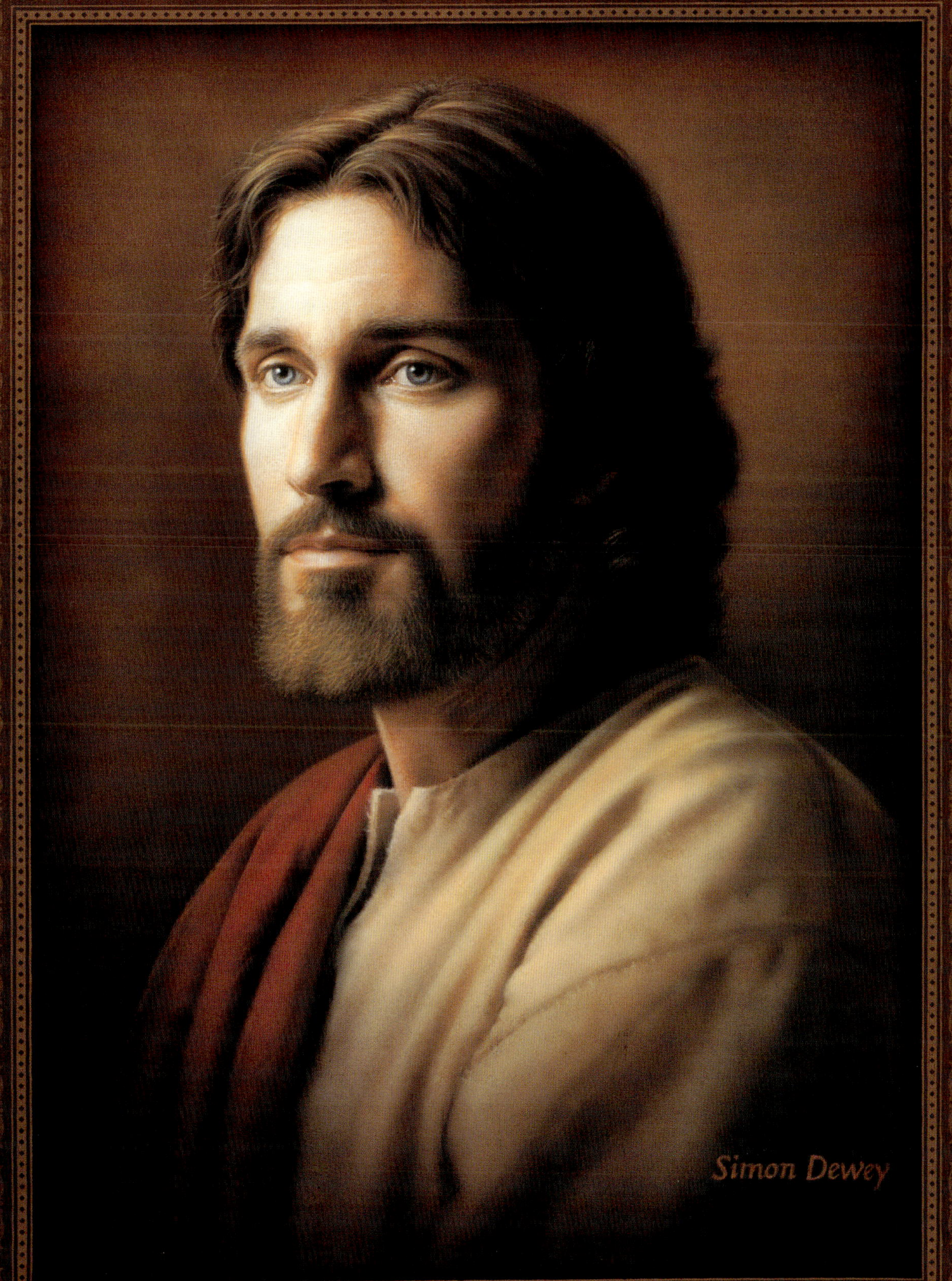
Simon Dewey

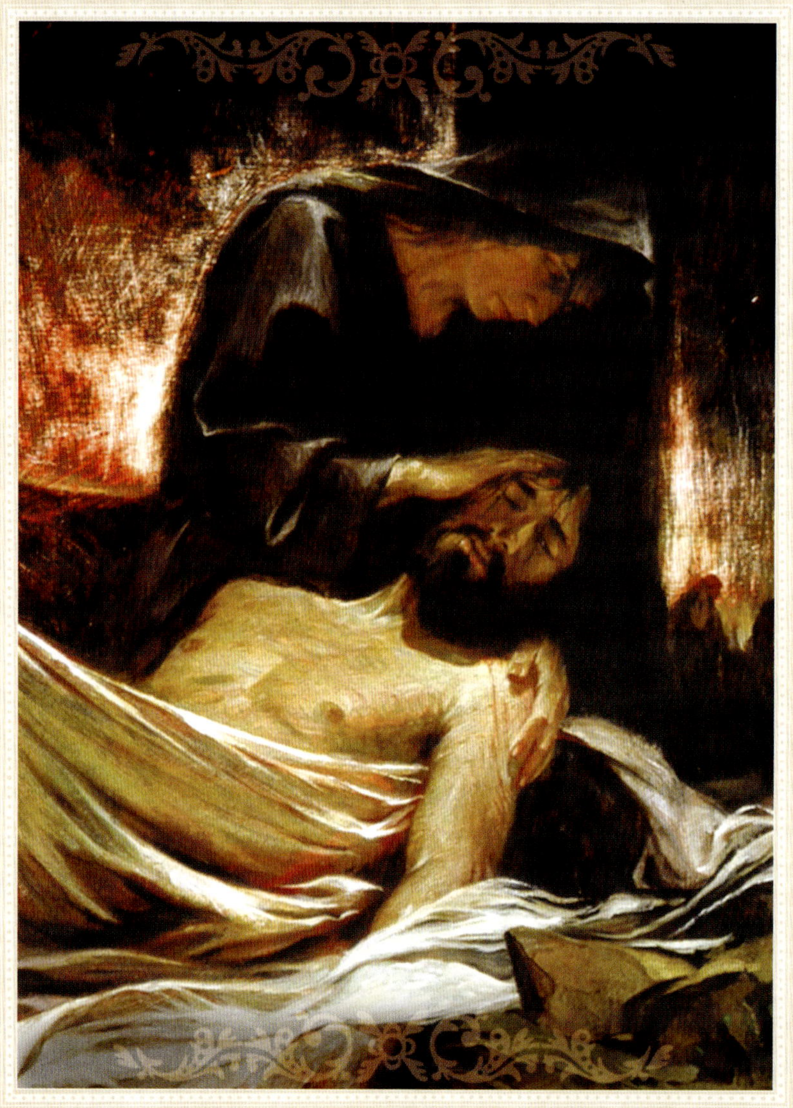

JOHN THE BELOVED DECLARED, "BEHOLD THE LAMB OF GOD, who taketh away the sin of the world!" What power! Only the Master Healer could take away the sin of the world. Our debt to Him is incalculably great.

Russell M. Nelson, "Jesus Christ—The Master Healer," *Ensign*, November 2005, 85

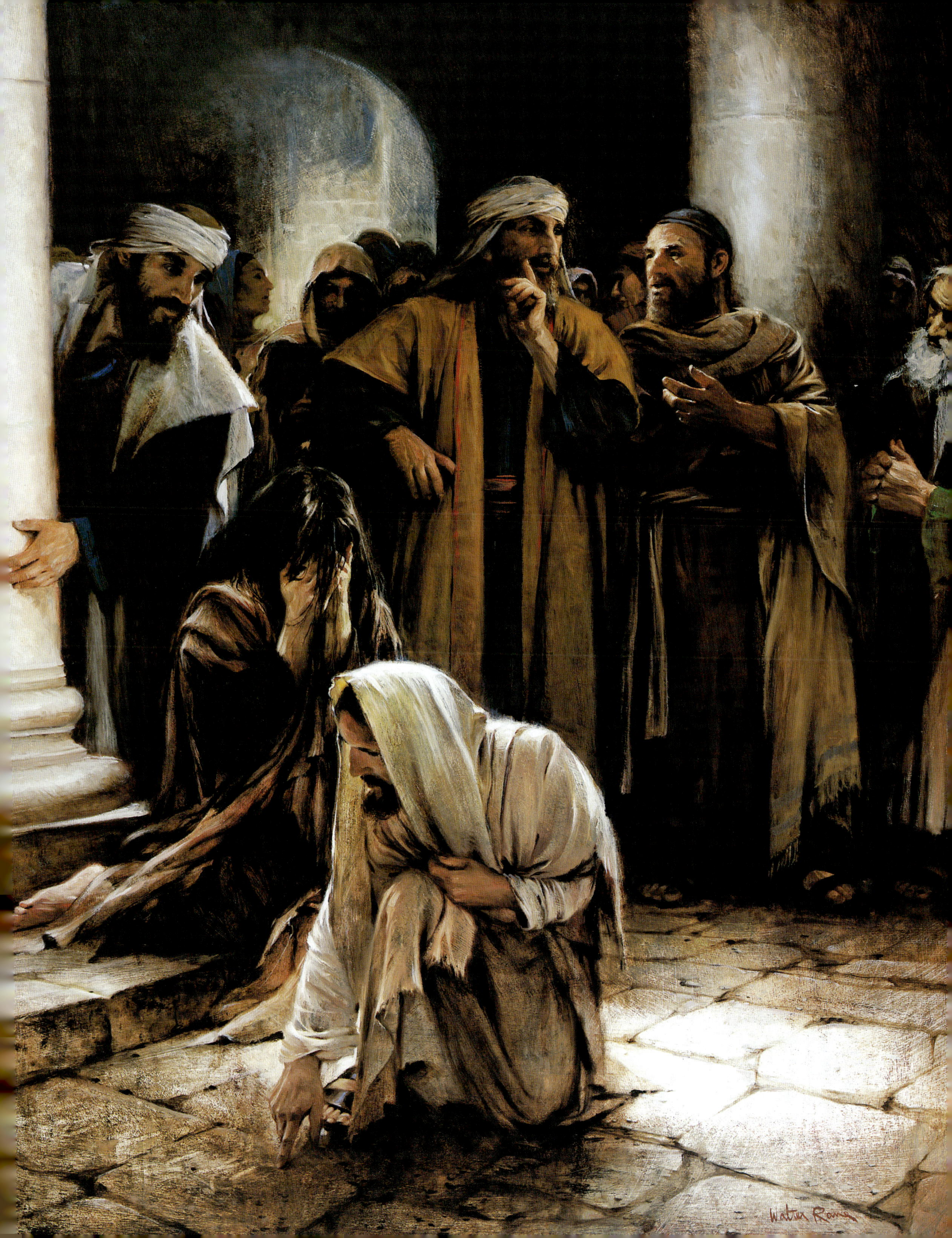
Walter Rane

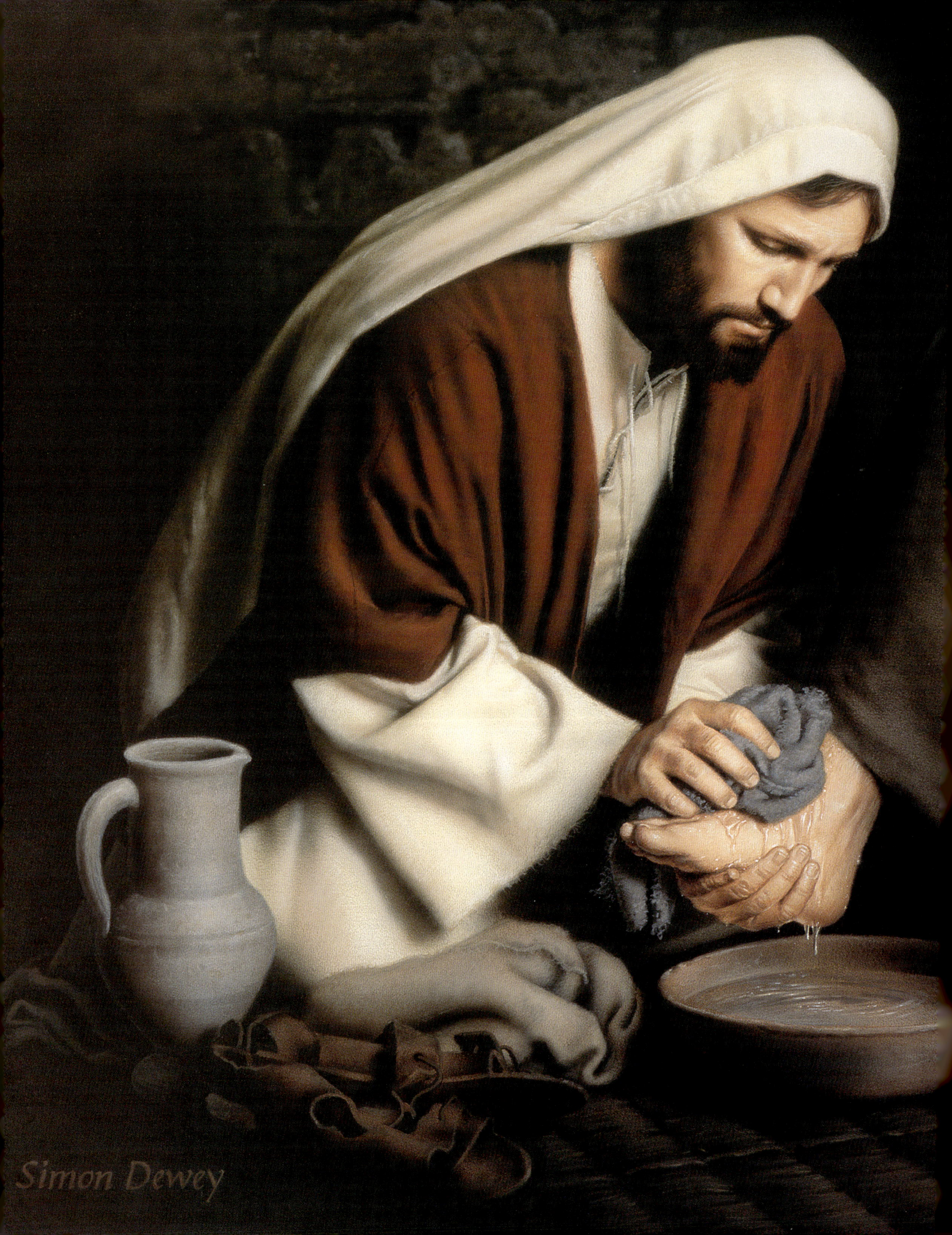
Simon Dewey

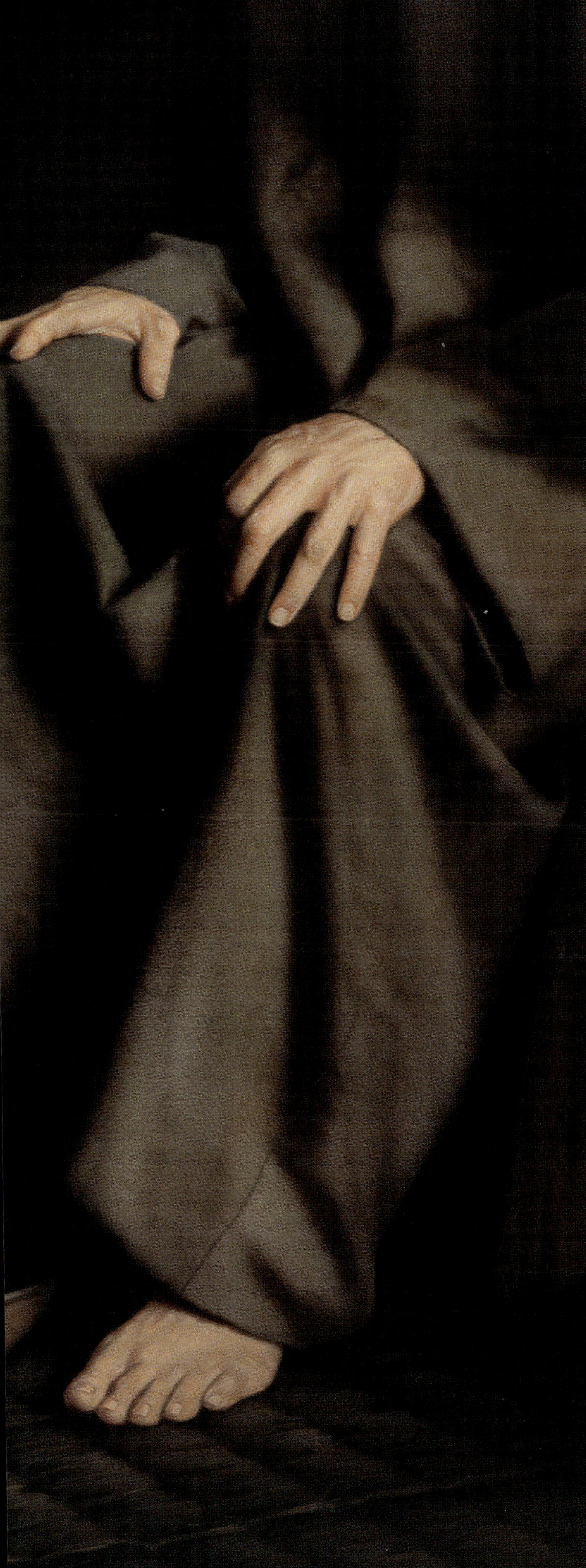

IT WAS THROUGH READING THE SCRIPTURES, and listening, that I could understand, at least in part, the power of the Atonement. Can you imagine how I felt when finally I could see that if I followed whatever conditions the Redeemer had set, I need never endure the agony of being spiritually unclean? Imagine the consoling, liberating, exalting feeling that will come to you when you see the reality of the Atonement and the practical everyday value of it to you individually.

Boyd K. Packer, "Washed Clean," *Ensign*, May 1997, 9

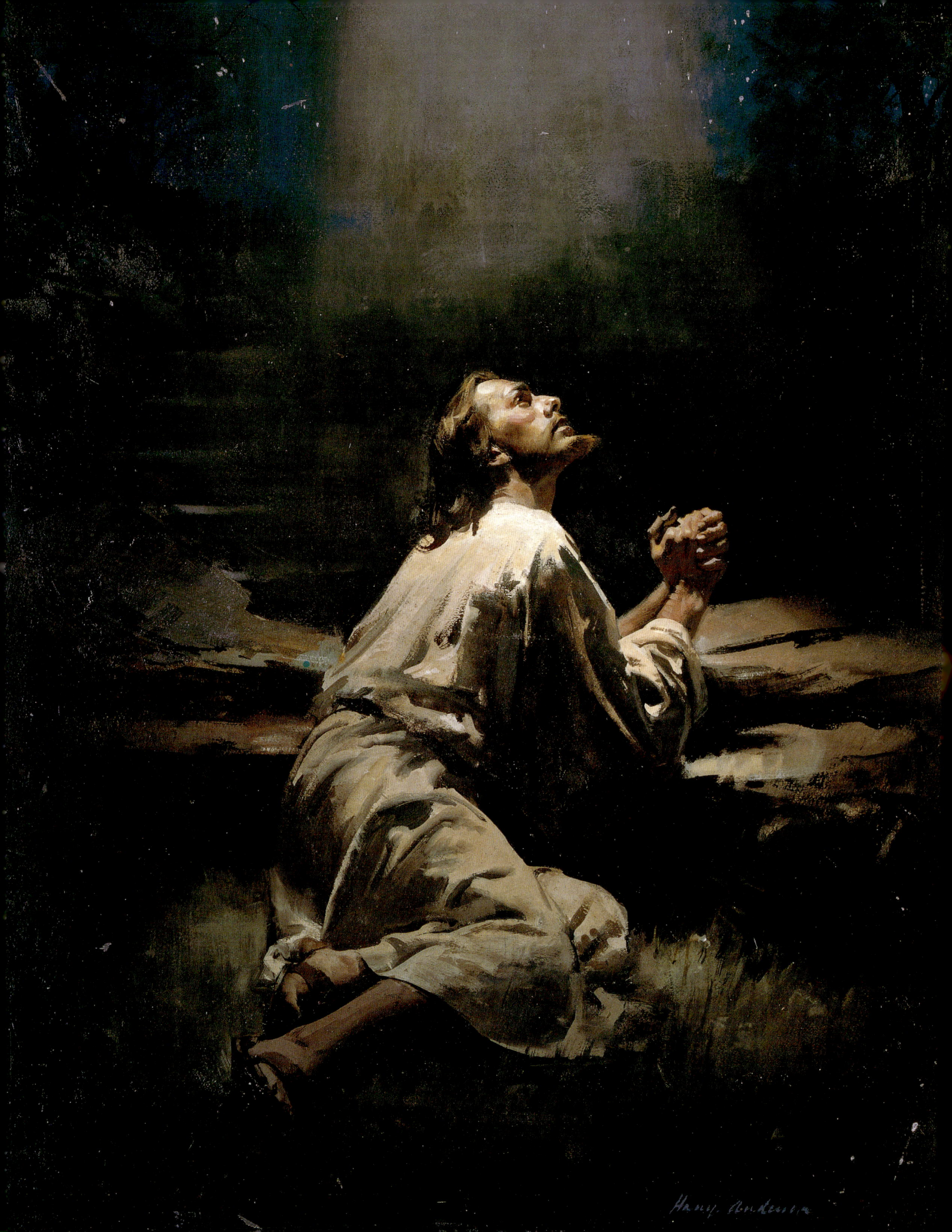

IT WAS . . . IN THE GARDEN OF GETHSEMANE, on that last night in mortality, that Jesus left His Apostles and descended alone into the depth of agony that would be His atoning sacrifice for the sins of all mankind. . . .

Is it any wonder that we walk quietly and reverently here? It is any wonder that we make sacred covenants because of the love that was demonstrated here? Is it any wonder that Christ, the greatest of all, partook of the bitter cup and did not shrink here, that we might not suffer if we would repent and come unto Him?

Jeffrey R. Holland, "Special Witnesses of Christ," *Ensign*, April 2001, 4

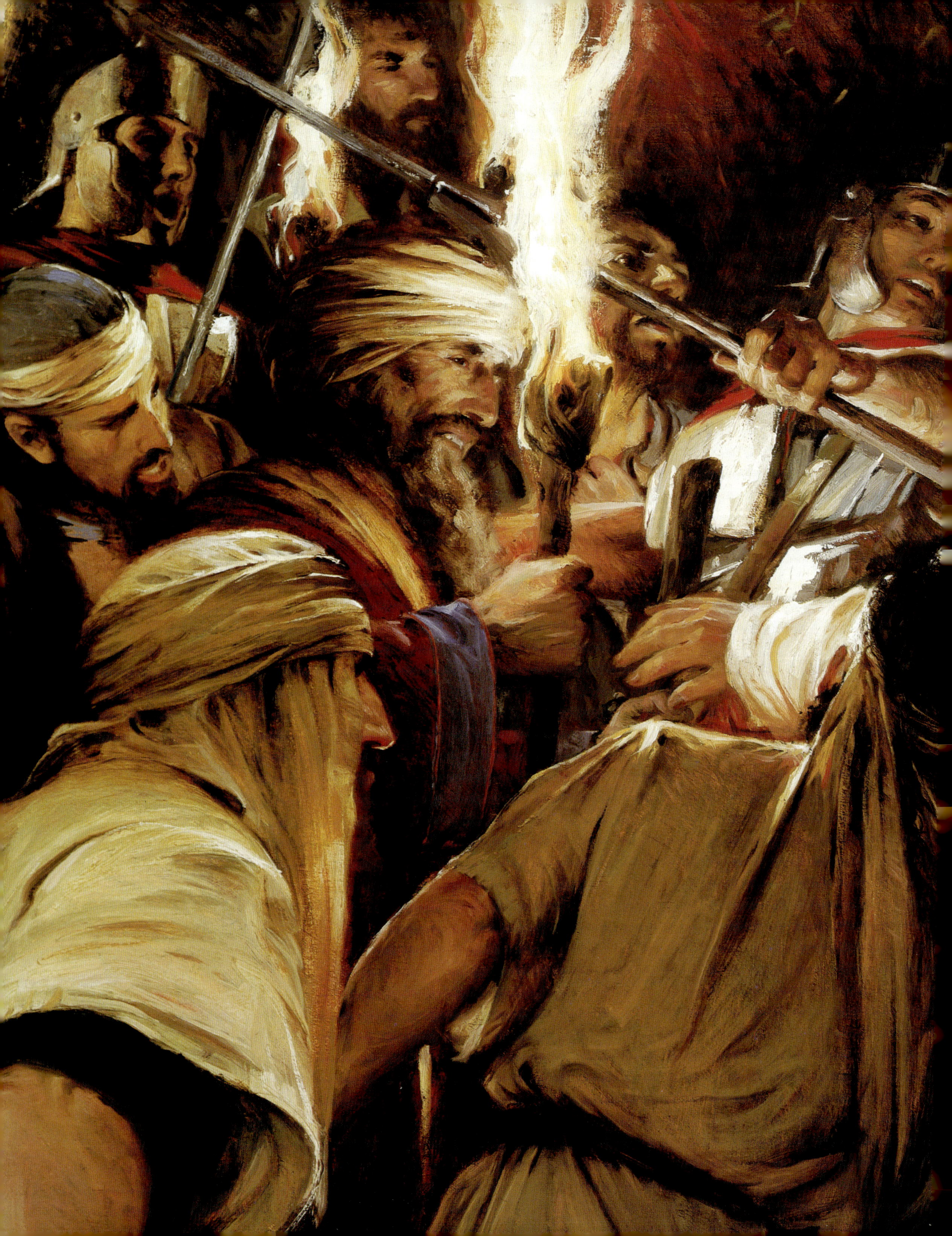

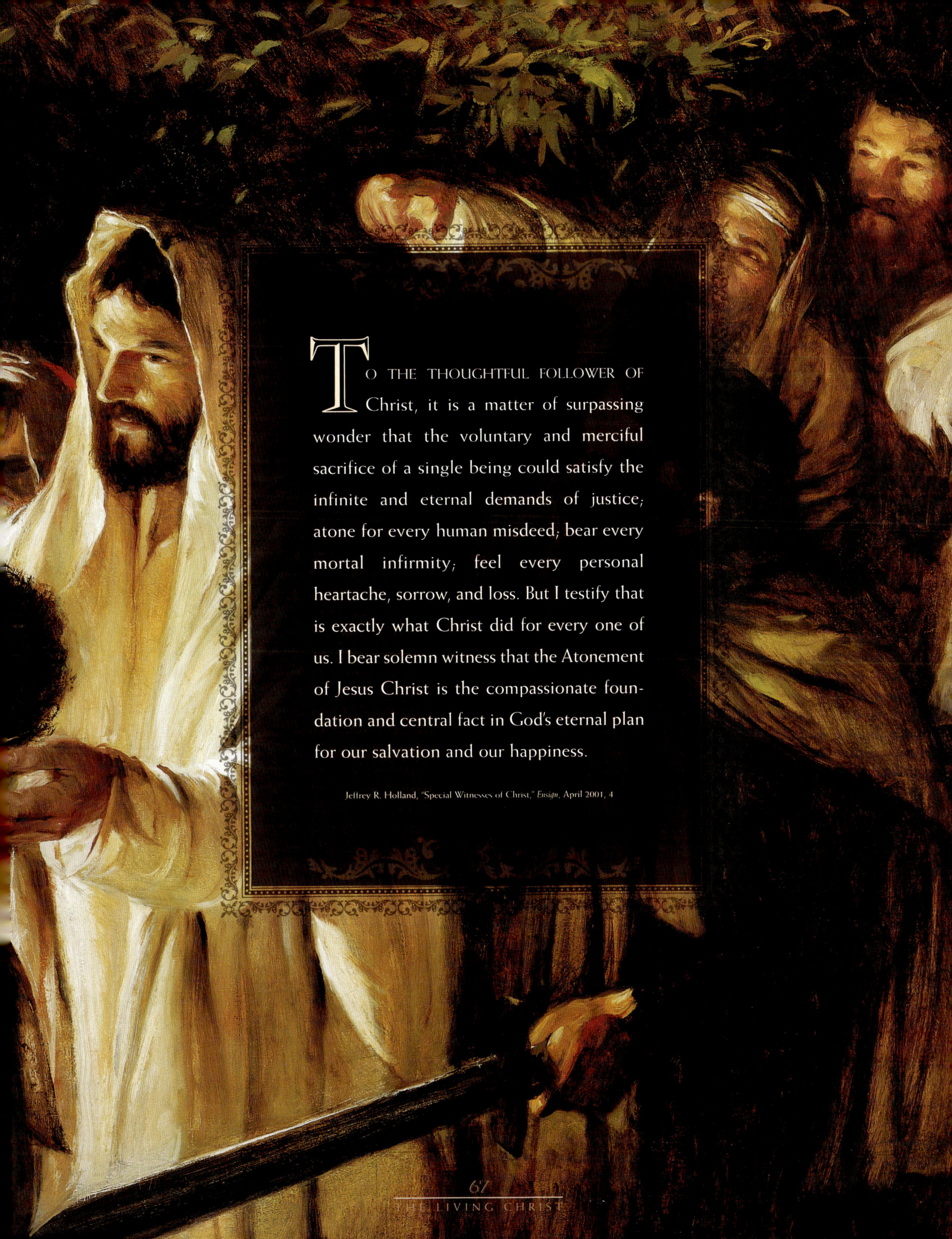

TO THE THOUGHTFUL FOLLOWER OF Christ, it is a matter of surpassing wonder that the voluntary and merciful sacrifice of a single being could satisfy the infinite and eternal demands of justice; atone for every human misdeed; bear every mortal infirmity; feel every personal heartache, sorrow, and loss. But I testify that is exactly what Christ did for every one of us. I bear solemn witness that the Atonement of Jesus Christ is the compassionate foundation and central fact in God's eternal plan for our salvation and our happiness.

Jeffrey R. Holland, "Special Witnesses of Christ," *Ensign*, April 2001, 4

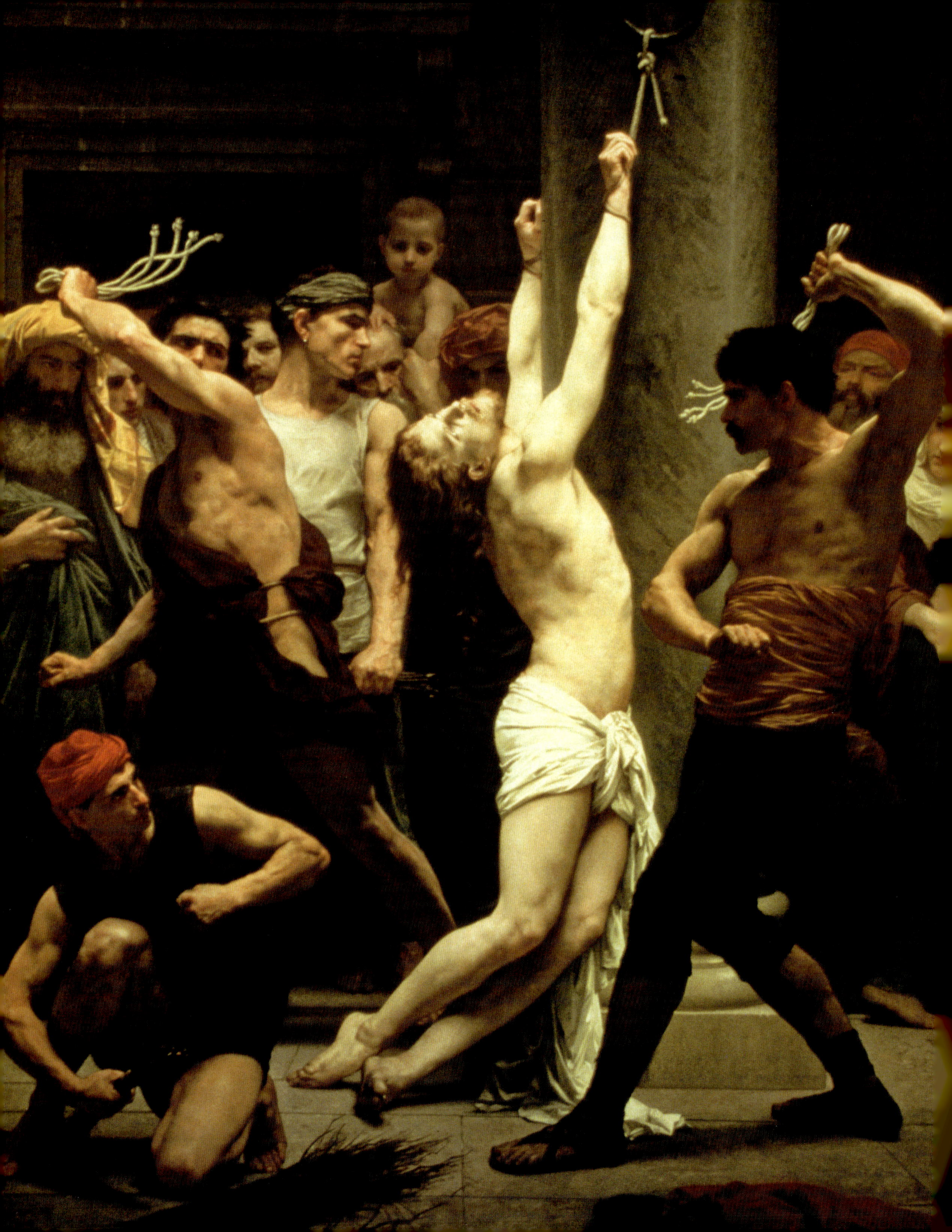

WE CANNOT, EVEN IN THE DEPTHS of disease, tell him anything at all about suffering. In ways we cannot comprehend, our sicknesses and infirmities were borne by him even before they were borne by us. The very weight of our combined sins caused him to descend below all. We have never been, nor will we be, in personal depths such as he has known. Thus, his atonement demonstrated and perfected his empathy and his capacity to succor us, for which we can be everlastingly grateful as he tutors us in our trials.

Neal A. Maxwell, "Our Acceptance of Christ," *Ensign*, June 1984, 69

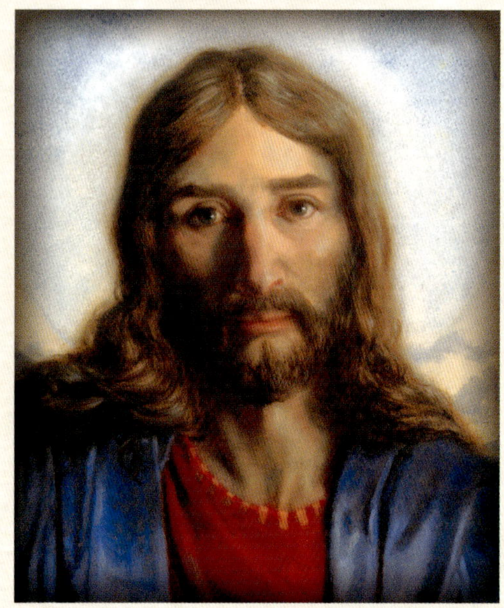

JESUS COULD HAVE CALLED UPON LEGIONS of angels to bring Him down from the cross, but He did not. He endured to the end that we would have the benefits of the atoning sacrifice; that mercy could be brought into the world; that justice would be satisfied; that we might be resurrected; and that we might be able to earn, through our obedience, eternal life in the presence of God the Father and Jesus Christ.

Robert D. Hales, "Lessons from the Atonement That Help Us to Endure to the End," *Ensign*, November 1985, 18

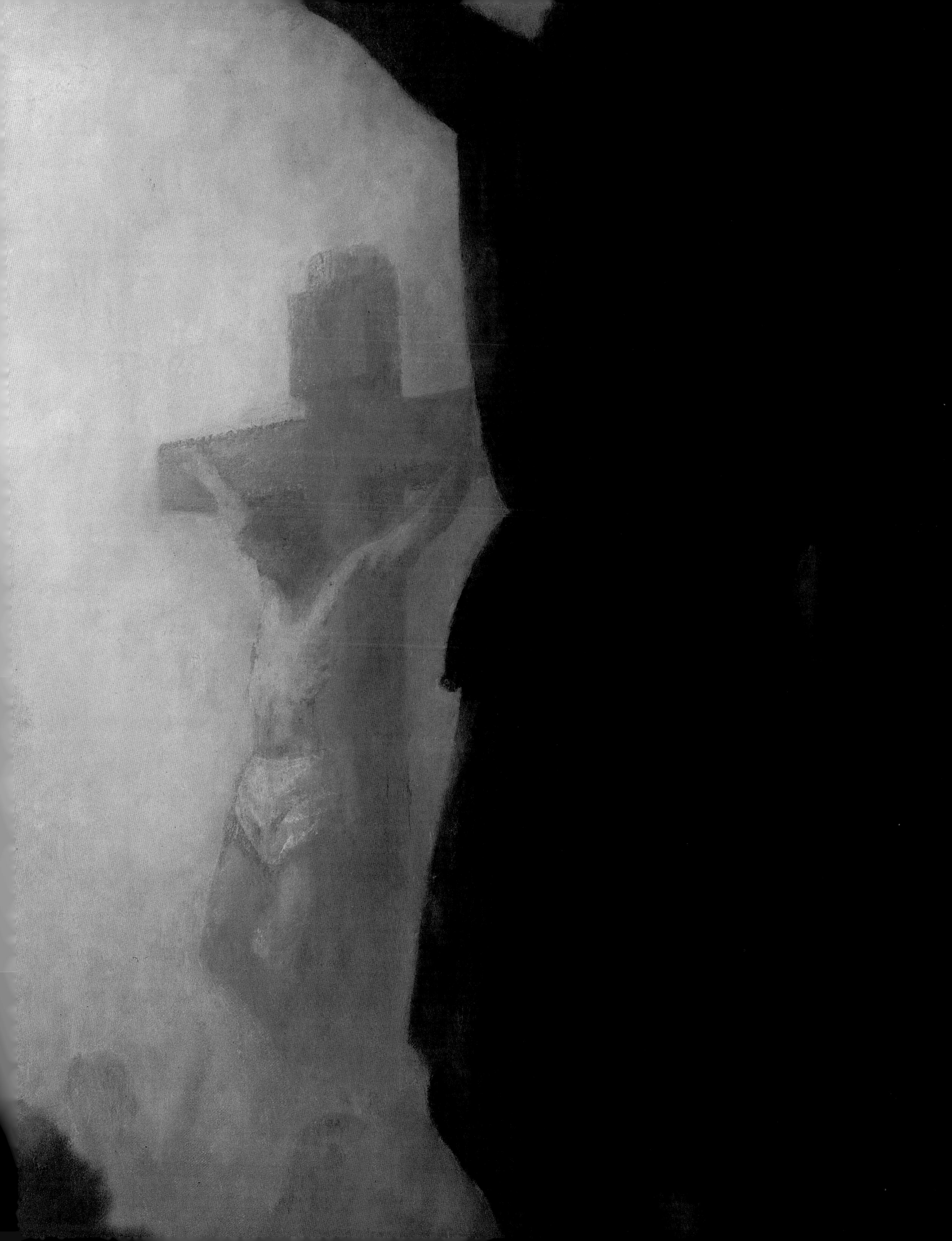

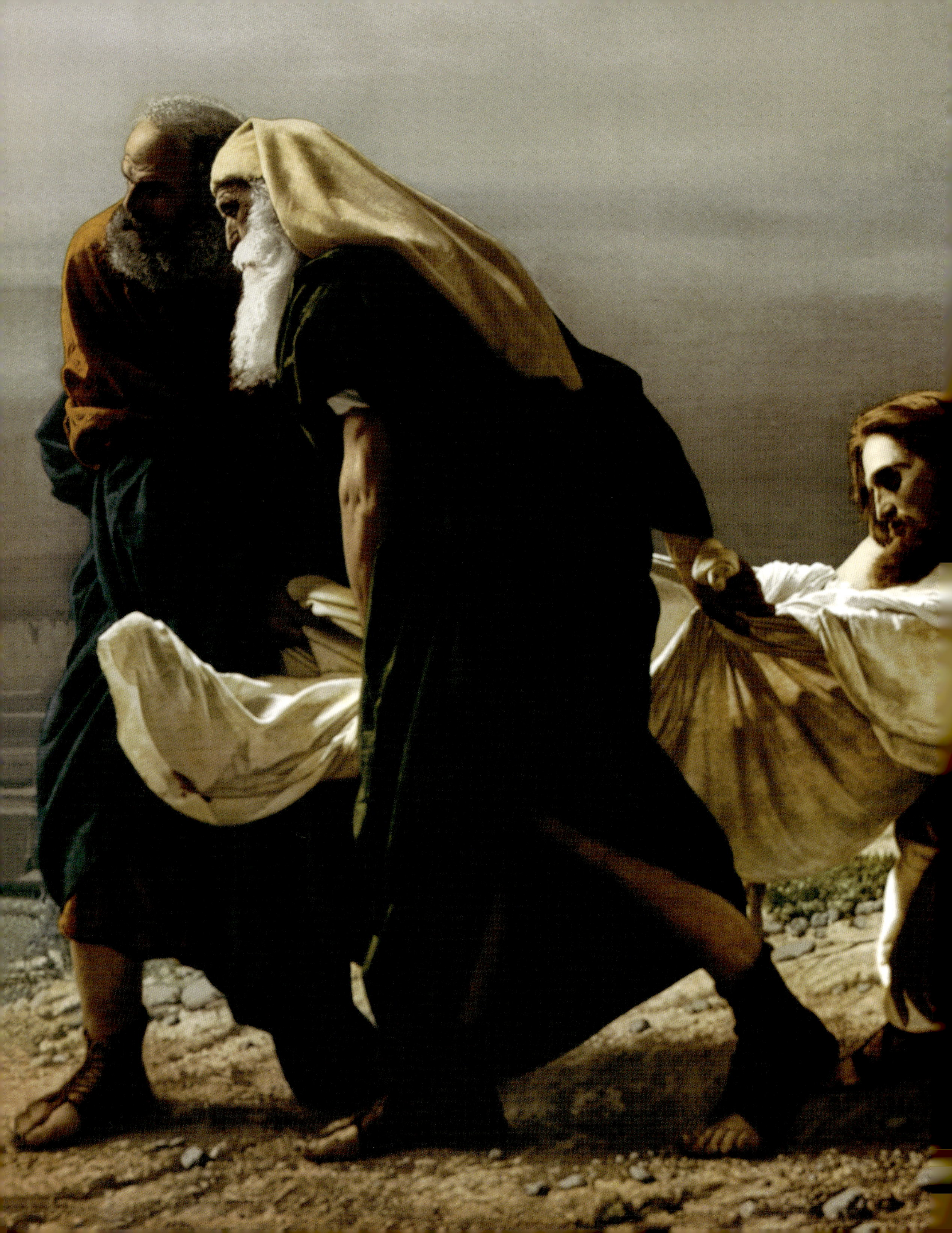

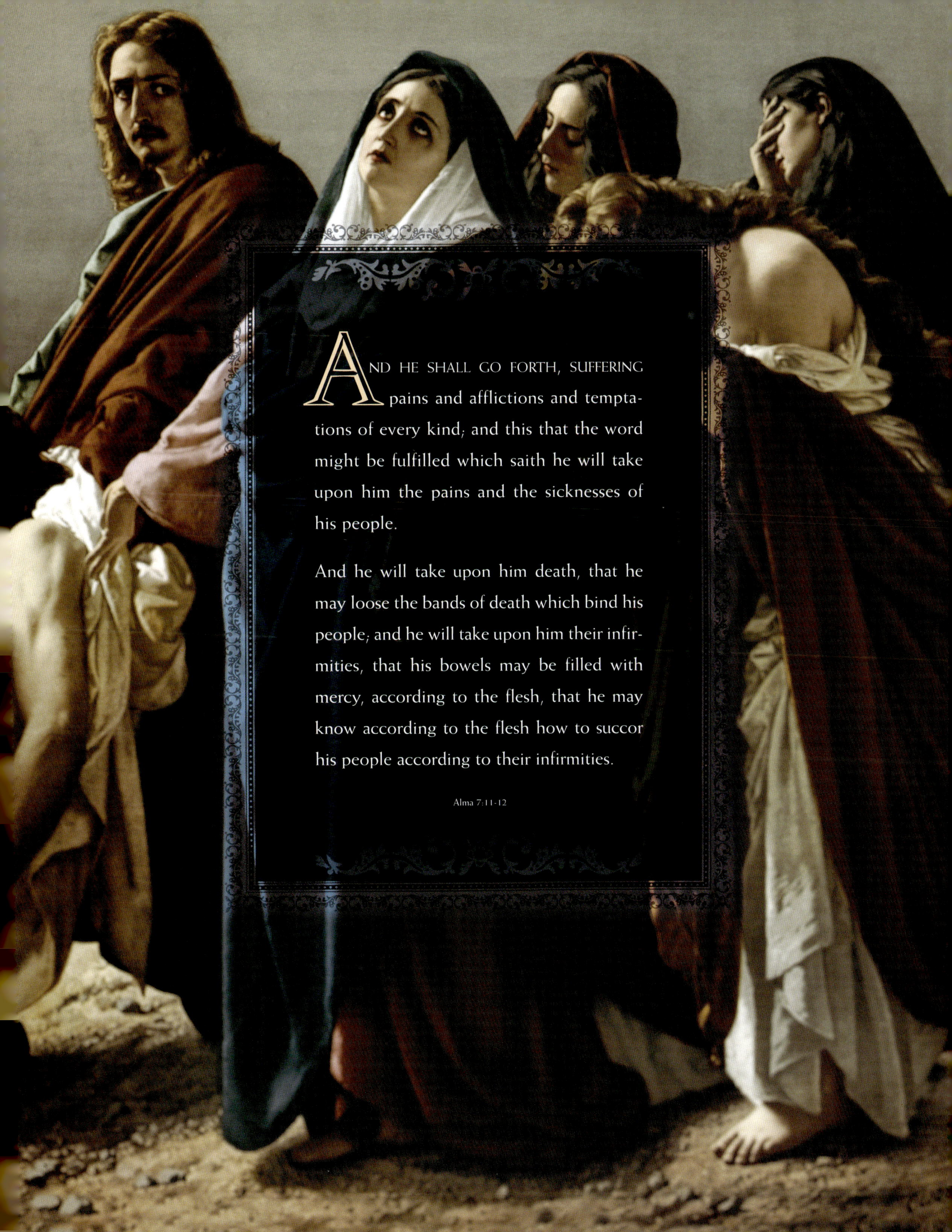

And he shall go forth, suffering pains and afflictions and temptations of every kind; and this that the word might be fulfilled which saith he will take upon him the pains and the sicknesses of his people.

And he will take upon him death, that he may loose the bands of death which bind his people; and he will take upon him their infirmities, that his bowels may be filled with mercy, according to the flesh, that he may know according to the flesh how to succor his people according to their infirmities.

Alma 7:11-12

FROM THE TERRIBLE CONFLICT IN Gethsemane, Christ emerged a victor. Though in the dark tribulation of that fearful hour He had pleaded that the bitter cup be removed from His lips, the request, however oft repeated, was always conditional; the accomplishment of the Father's will was never lost sight of as the object of the Son's supreme desire.

James E. Talmage, *Jesus the Christ* (Salt Lake City: The Church of Jesus Christ of Latter-day Saints, 1973), 614

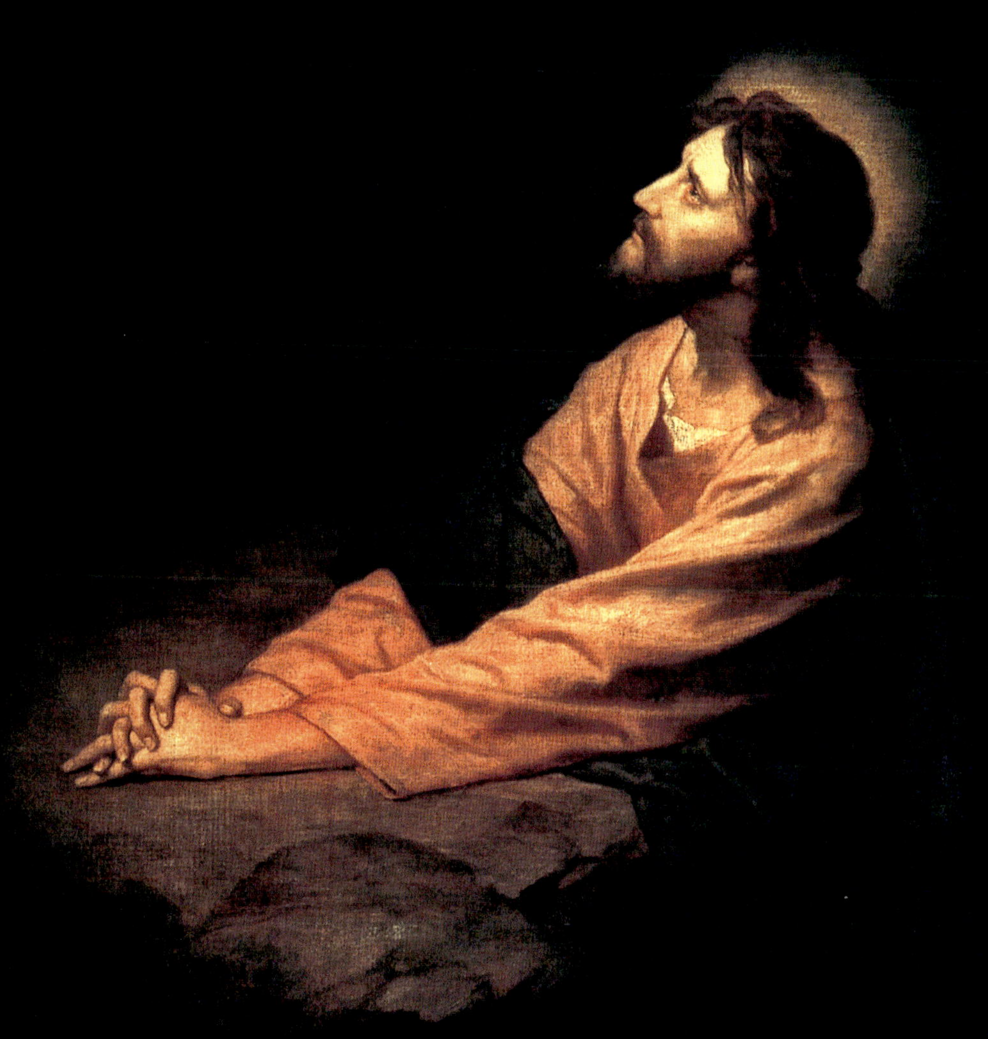

EVEN HE, IN THOSE MOMENTS THAT mattered so much, had to choose voluntarily to go through Gethsemane and to hang on the cross at Calvary. He taught us that there can be no growth without real freedom.

Spencer W. Kimball, "Jesus: The Perfect Leader," *Ensign*, August 1979, 5

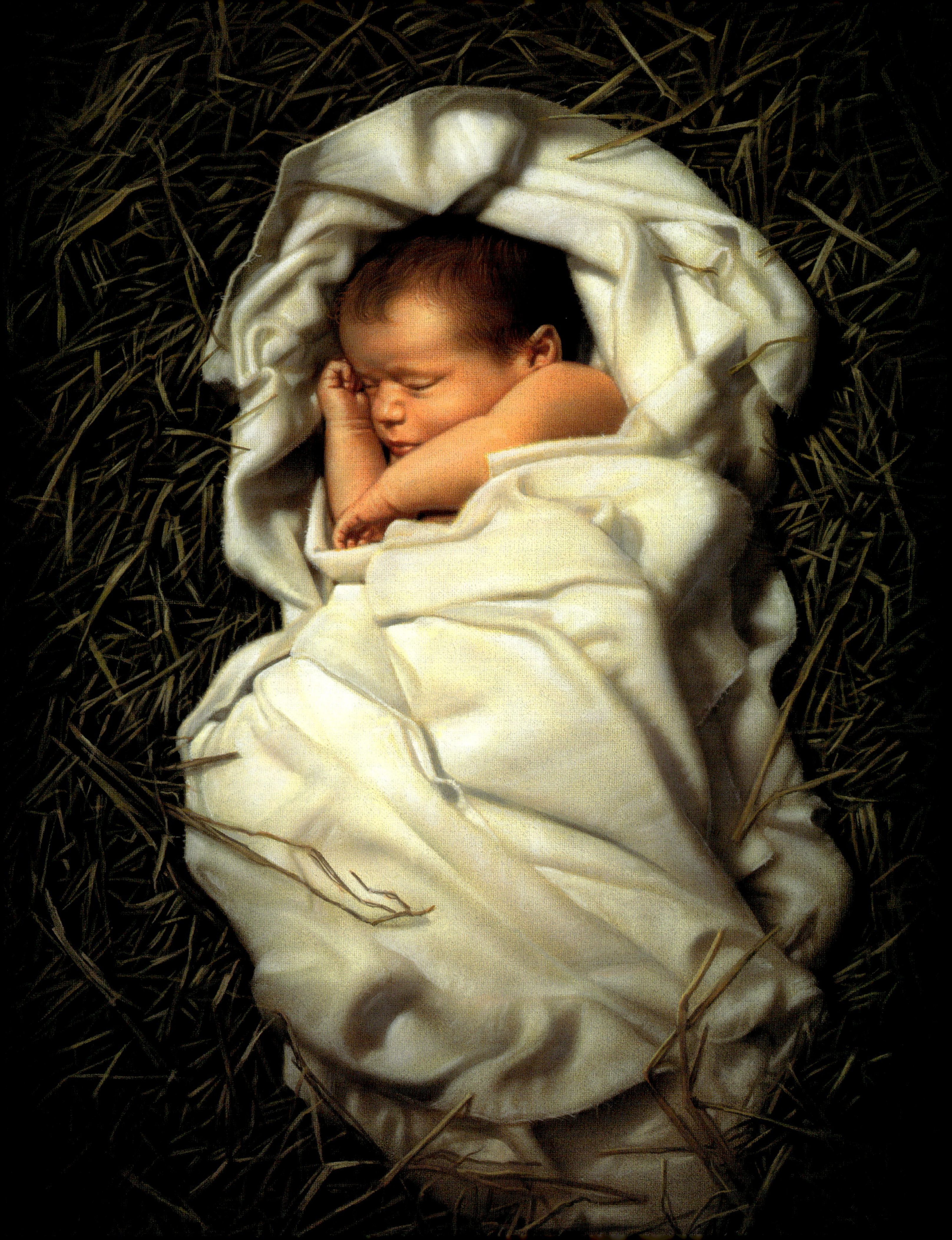

When we feel so alone, we cannot presume to teach him who, at the apogee of his agony, trod "the winepress alone" anything about feeling forsaken.

Neal A. Maxwell, "Our Acceptance of Christ," *Ensign*, June 1984, 69

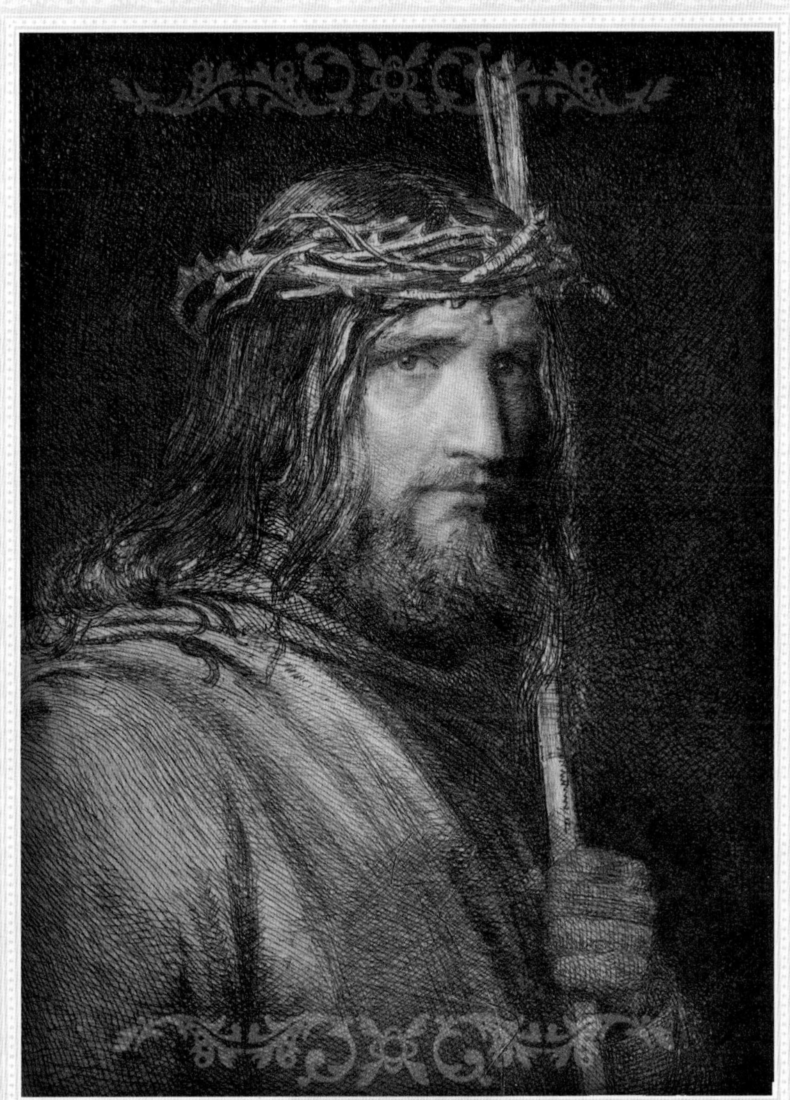

THE LONELINESS OF HIS BIRTH WAS TO BE, IN A SENSE, duplicated in the loneliness of his death. Foxes had holes and birds had nests, but the Son of Man had nowhere to lay his head either in his nativity or in his last hours of mortality.

Howard W. Hunter, "Christ, Our Passover," *Ensign*, May 1985, 17

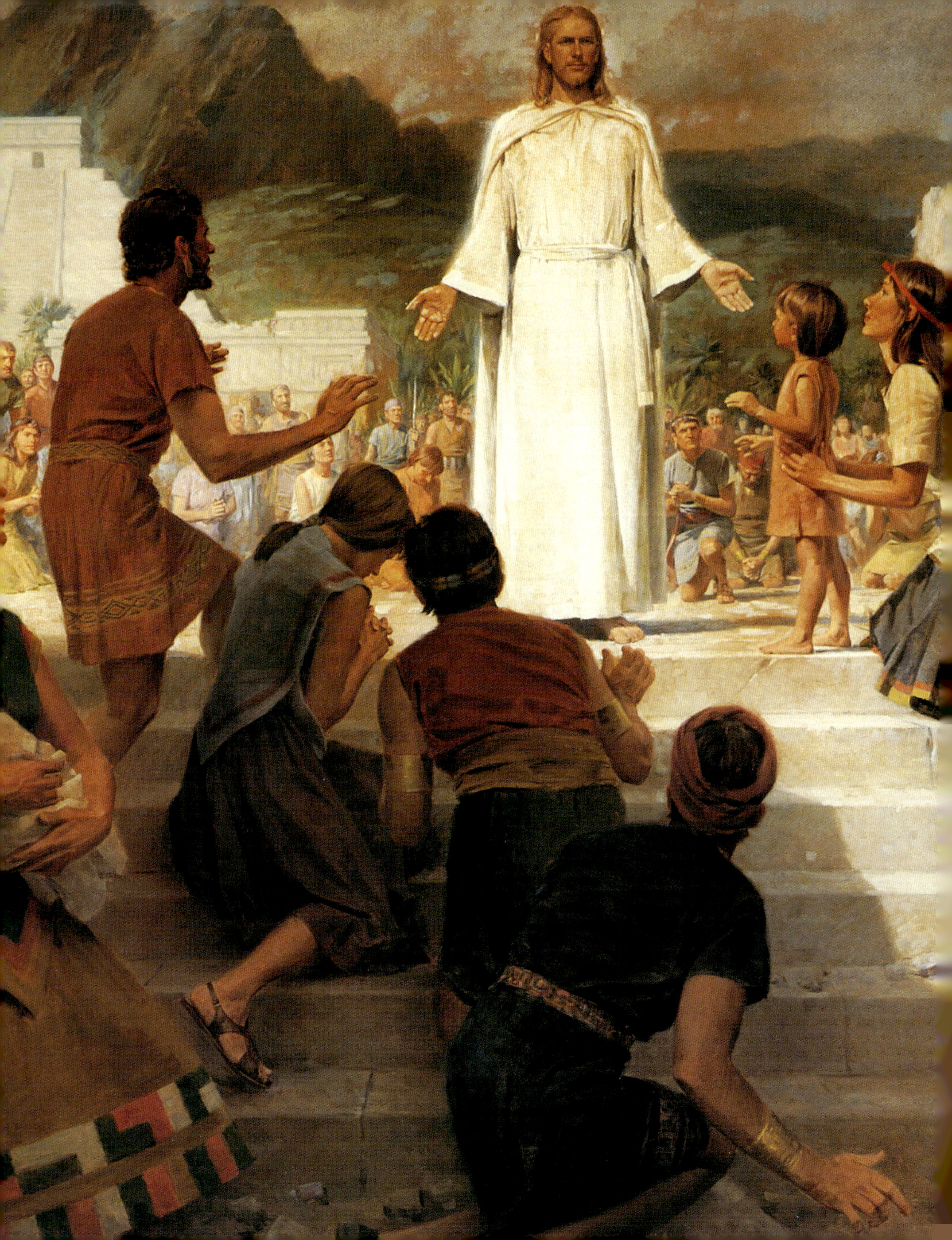

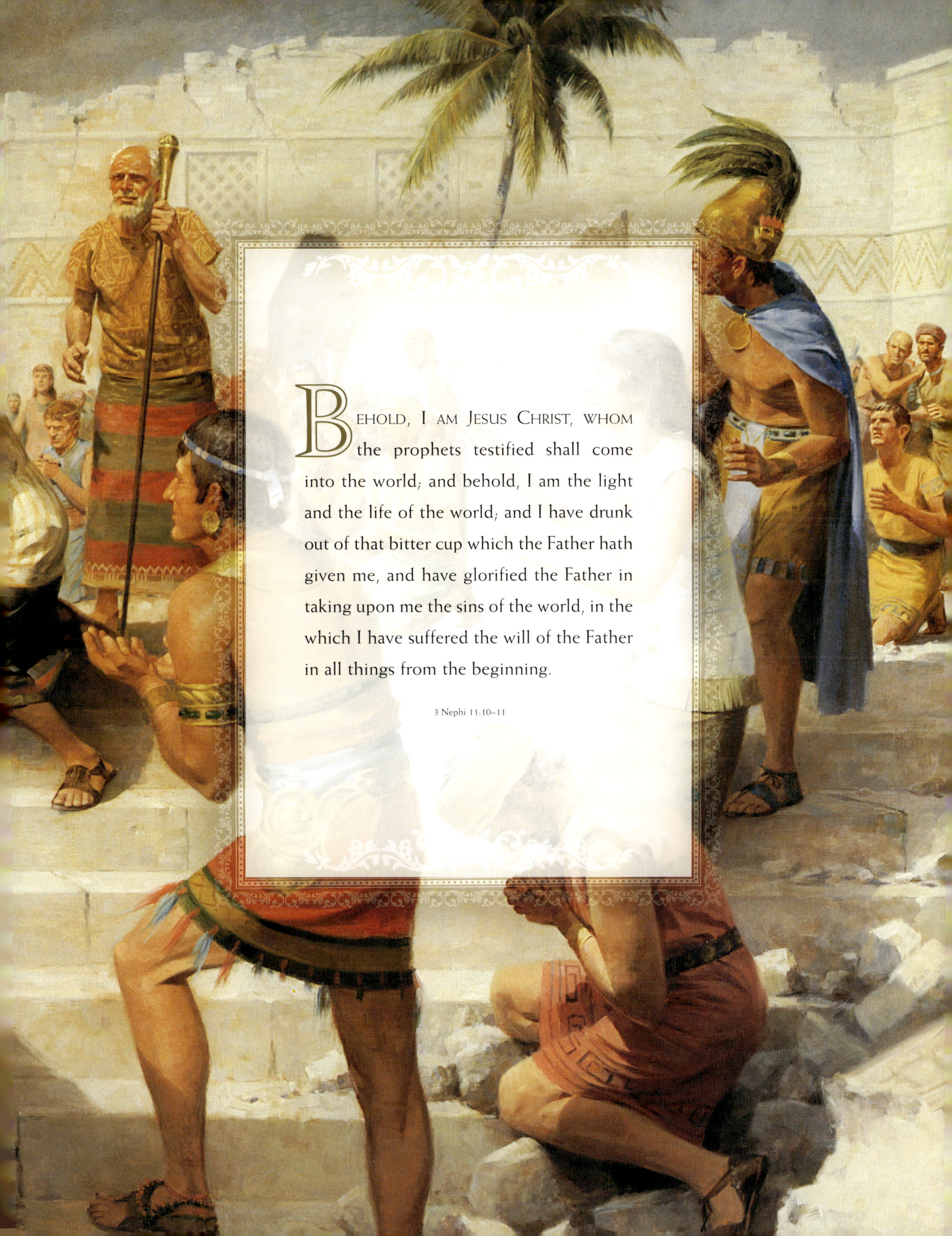

BEHOLD, I AM JESUS CHRIST, WHOM the prophets testified shall come into the world; and behold, I am the light and the life of the world; and I have drunk out of that bitter cup which the Father hath given me, and have glorified the Father in taking upon me the sins of the world, in the which I have suffered the will of the Father in all things from the beginning.

3 Nephi 11:10–11

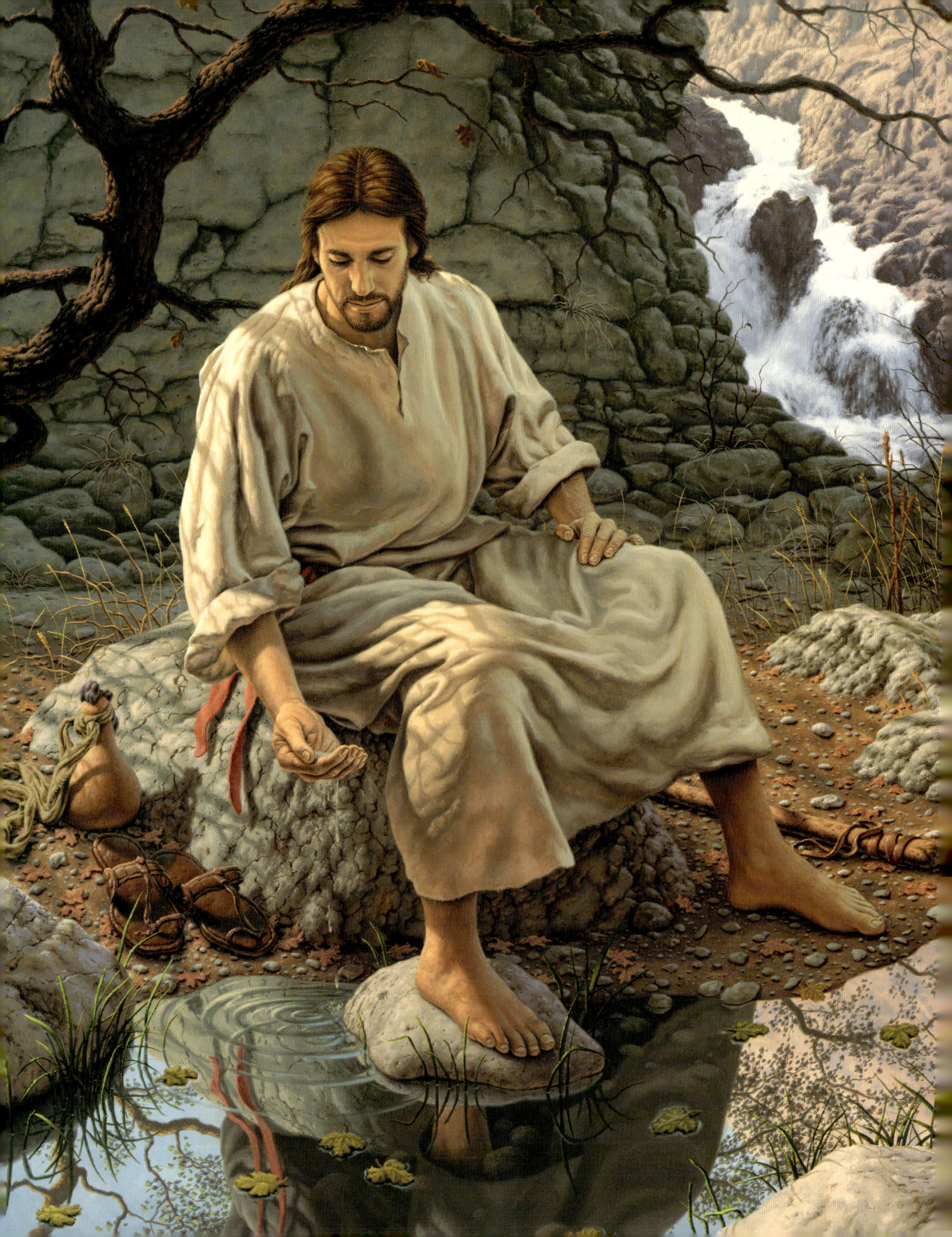

JESUS CHRIST POSSESSED *MERITS* THAT NO other child of Heavenly Father could possibly have. He was a God, Jehovah, before His birth in Bethlehem. His Father not only gave Him His spirit body but Jesus was His Only Begotten Son in the flesh. Our Master lived a perfect, sinless life and therefore was free from the demands of justice. He was and is perfect in every attribute, including love, compassion, patience, obedience, forgiveness, and humility. His *mercy* pays our debt to justice when we repent and obey Him. Even with our best efforts to obey His teachings we will still fall short, yet because of His *grace* we will be saved "after all we can do."

Richard G. Scott, "Jesus Christ, Our Redeemer," *Ensign*, May 1997, 53

OUR RESURRECTED LORD

On Calvary he was the dying Jesus. From the tomb he emerged **THE LIVING CHRIST.** *The cross had been the bitter fruit of Judas' betrayal, the summary of Peter's denial. The empty tomb now became the testimony of His divinity, the assurance of eternal life, the answer to Job's unanswered question: "If a man die, shall he live again?" (Job 14:14.)*

—Gordon B. Hinckley, "The Symbol of Christ," *Ensign*, May 1975, 92

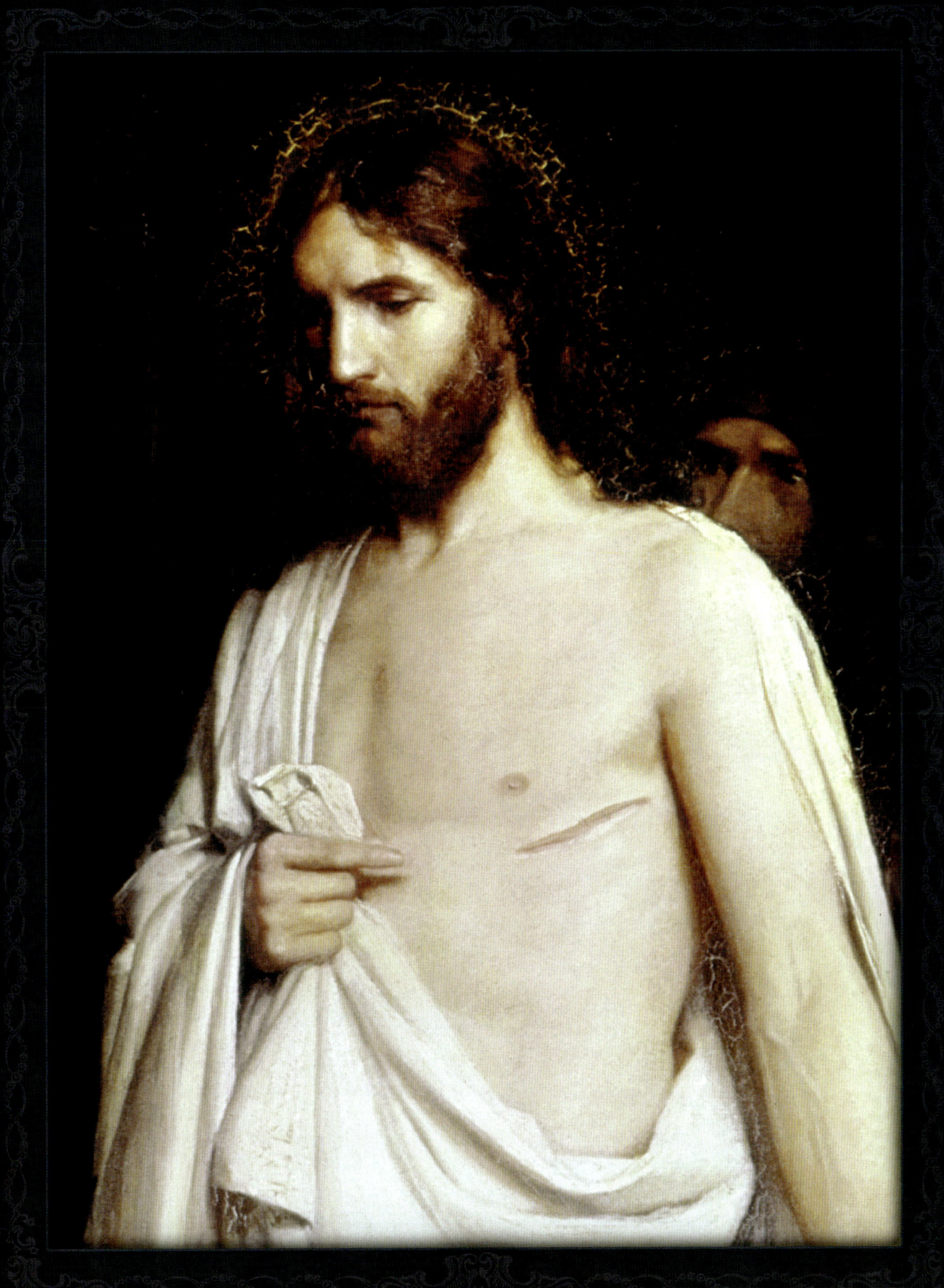

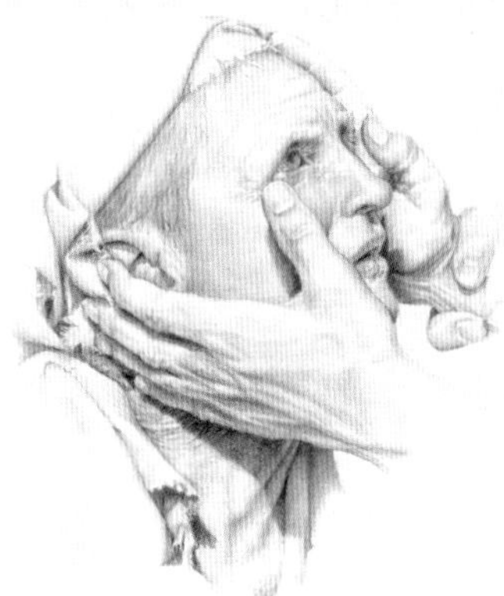

THE GIFT OF RESURRECTION IS THE LORD'S consummate act of healing. Thanks to Him, each body will be restored to its proper and perfect frame. Thanks to Him, no condition is hopeless. Thanks to Him, brighter days are ahead, both here and hereafter. Real joy awaits each of us—on the other side of sorrow.

Russell M. Nelson, "Jesus Christ—the Master Healer," *Ensign*, November 2005, 85

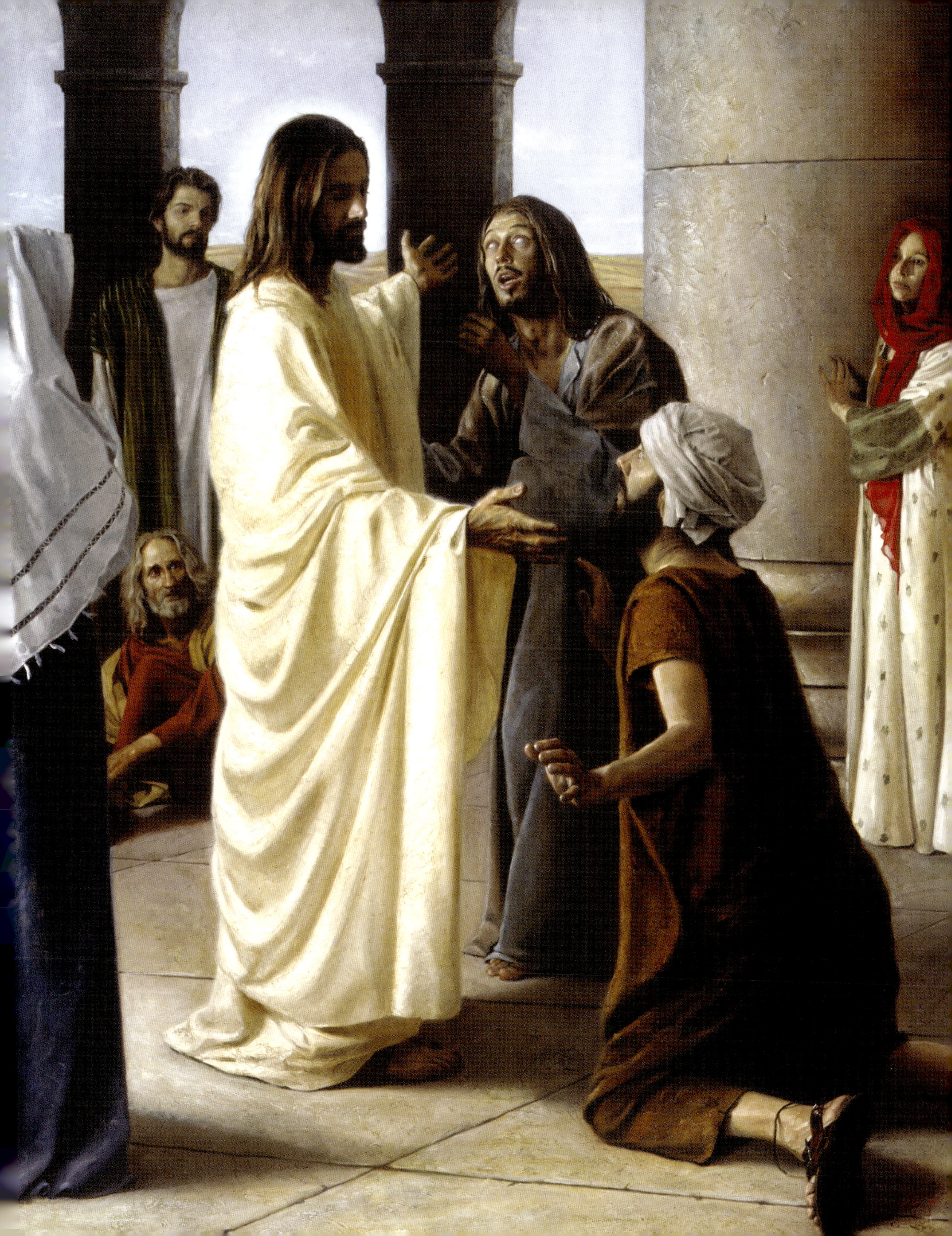

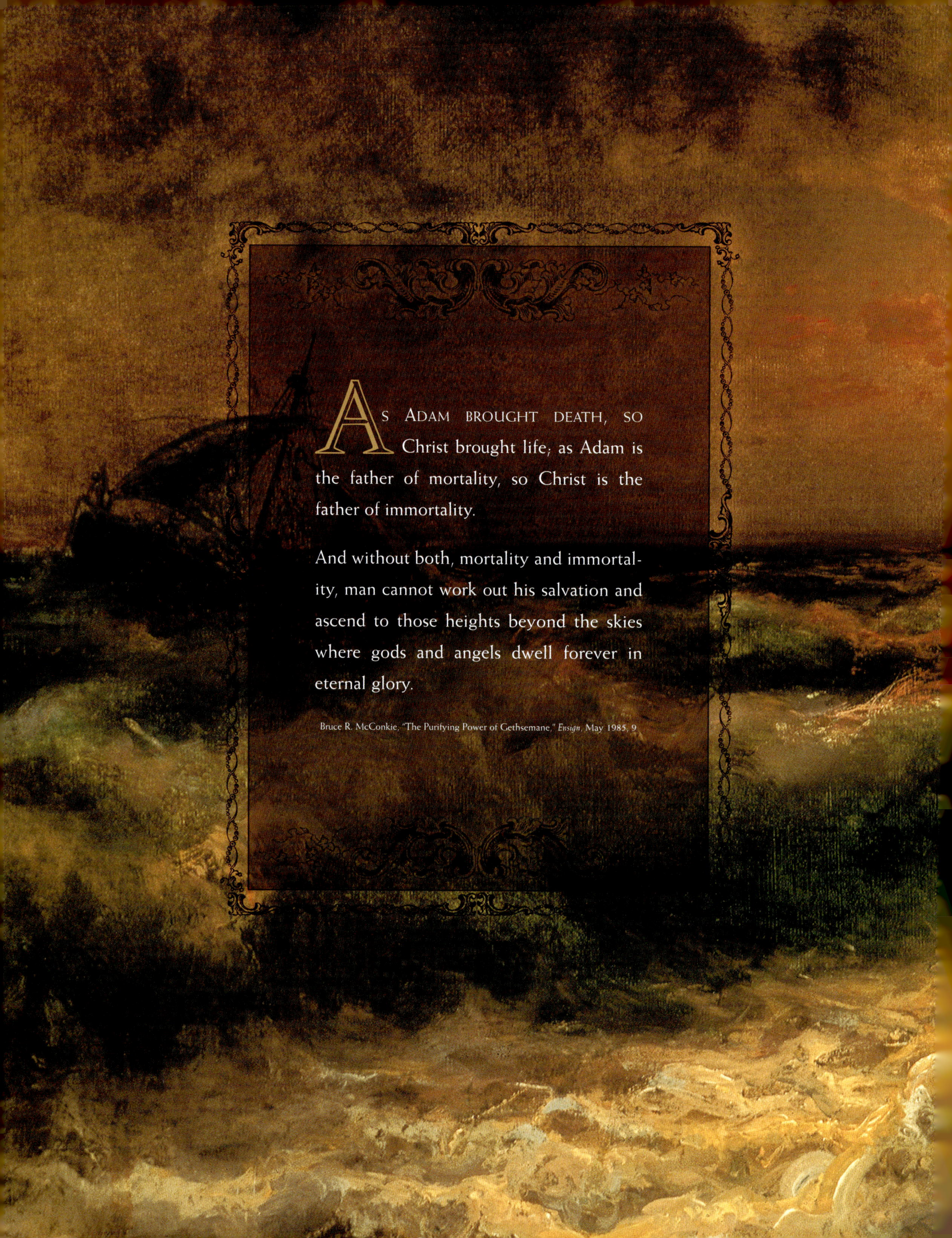

As Adam brought death, so Christ brought life; as Adam is the father of mortality, so Christ is the father of immortality.

And without both, mortality and immortality, man cannot work out his salvation and ascend to those heights beyond the skies where gods and angels dwell forever in eternal glory.

Bruce R. McConkie, "The Purifying Power of Gethsemane," *Ensign*, May 1985, 9

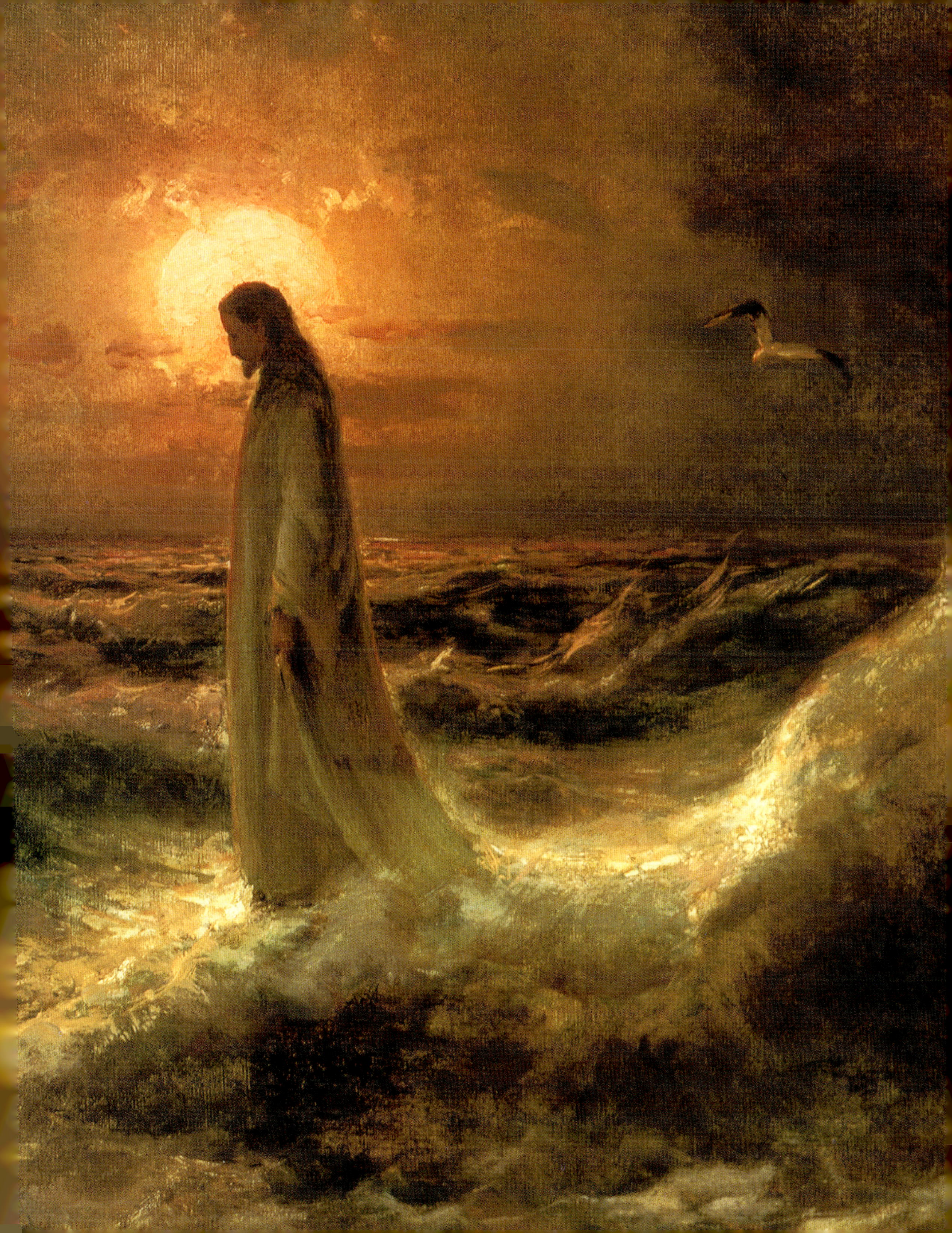

IT WAS THUS THROUGH THE ATONEMENT of Jesus Christ, the Father's Only Begotten Son in the flesh, that death was overcome, making possible the glorious resurrection. Jesus inherited immortality, power over death, from God, the Father, but from his mortal mother, Mary, the power to die. Christ's unique status meant that he gave his life voluntarily, that we might live!

Neal A. Maxwell, "Our Acceptance of Christ," *Ensign*, June 1984, 69

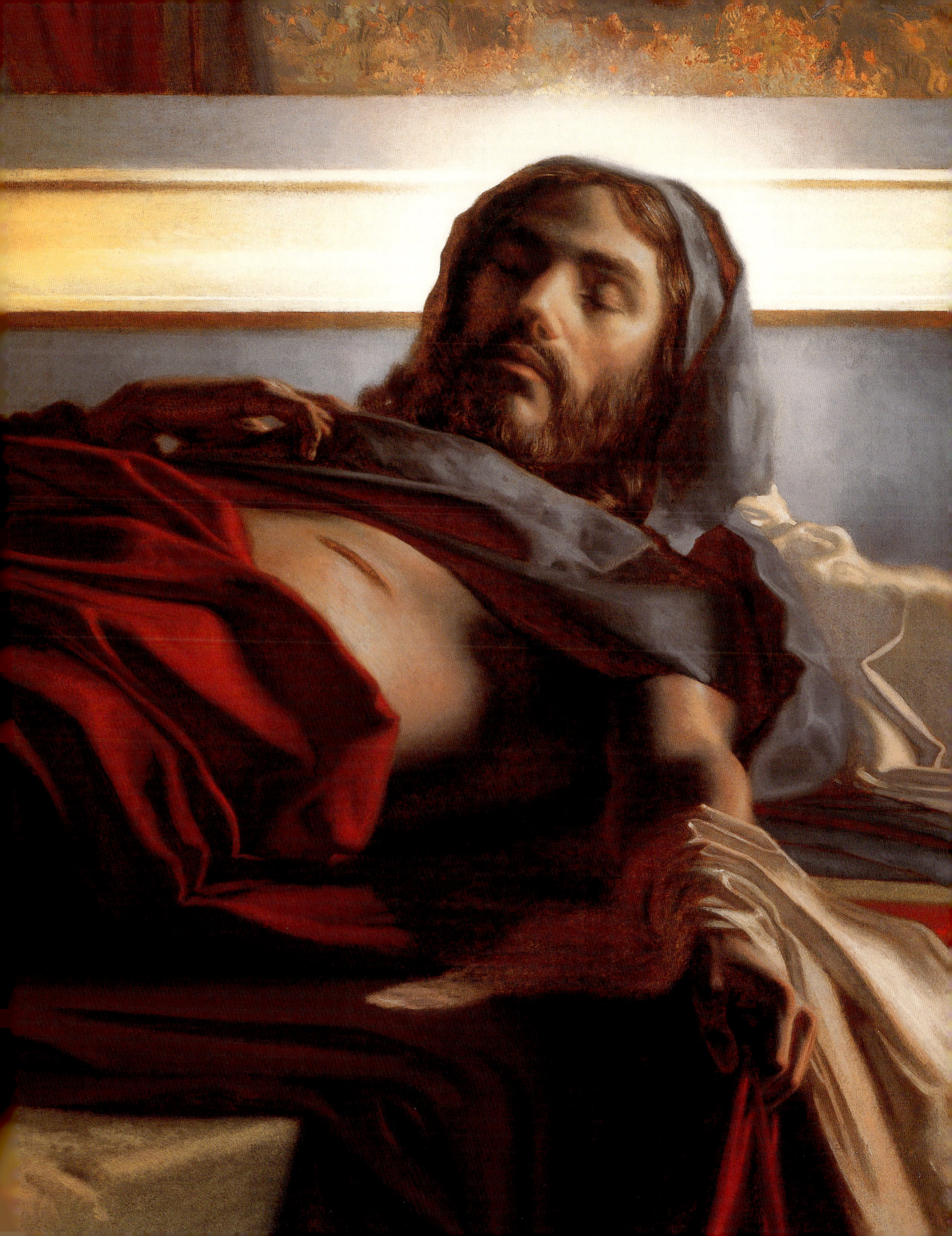

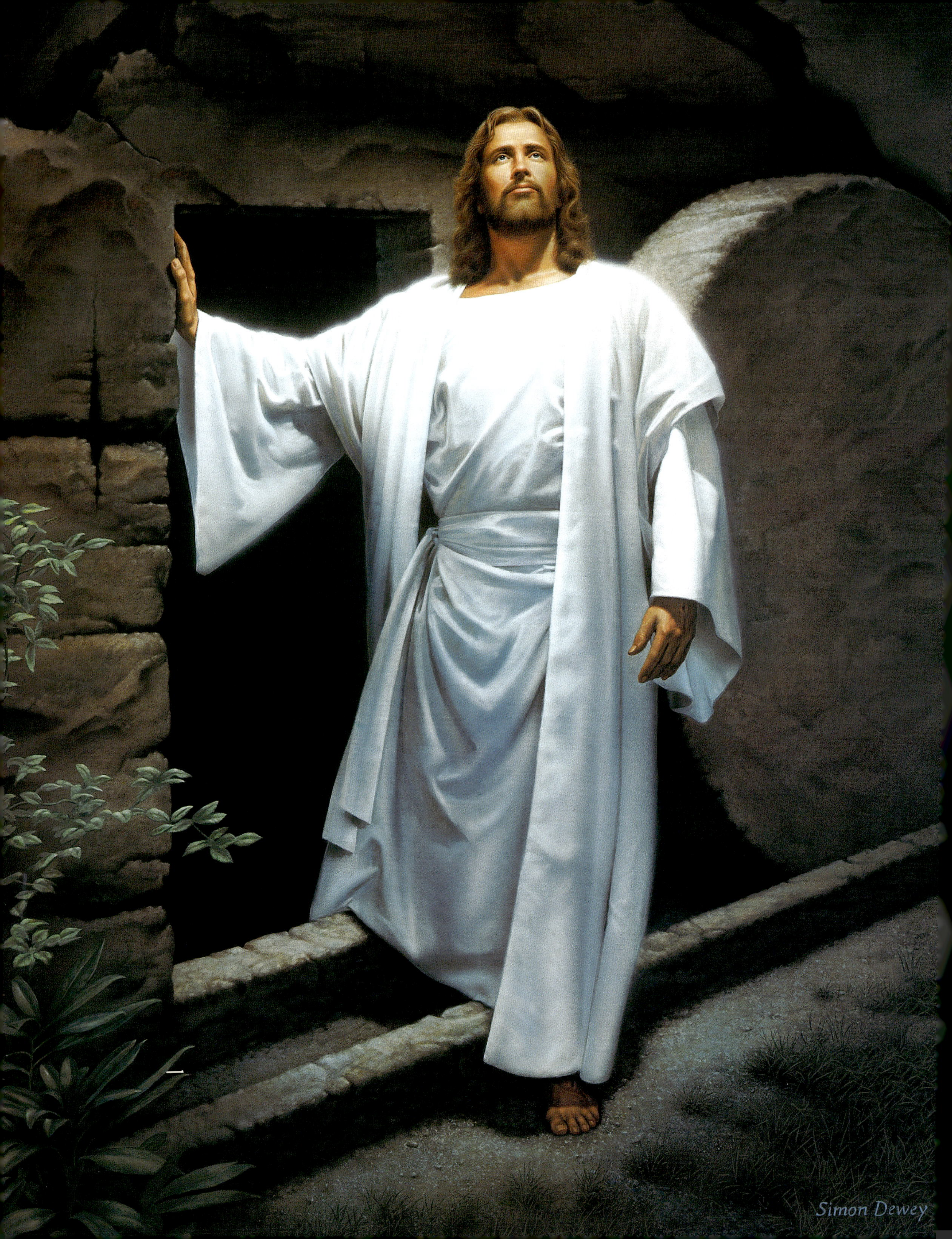
Simon Dewey

THE RESURRECTION OF JESUS CHRIST was the great crowning event of His life and mission. It was the capstone of the Atonement. The sacrifice of His life for all mankind was not complete without His coming forth from the grave, with the certainty of the Resurrection for all who have walked the earth.

Of all the victories in the chronicles of humanity, none is so great, none so universal in its effects, none so everlasting in its consequences as the victory of the crucified Lord, who came forth from the tomb that first Easter morning.

Gordon B. Hinckley, "Special Witnesses of Christ," *Ensign*, April 2001, 4

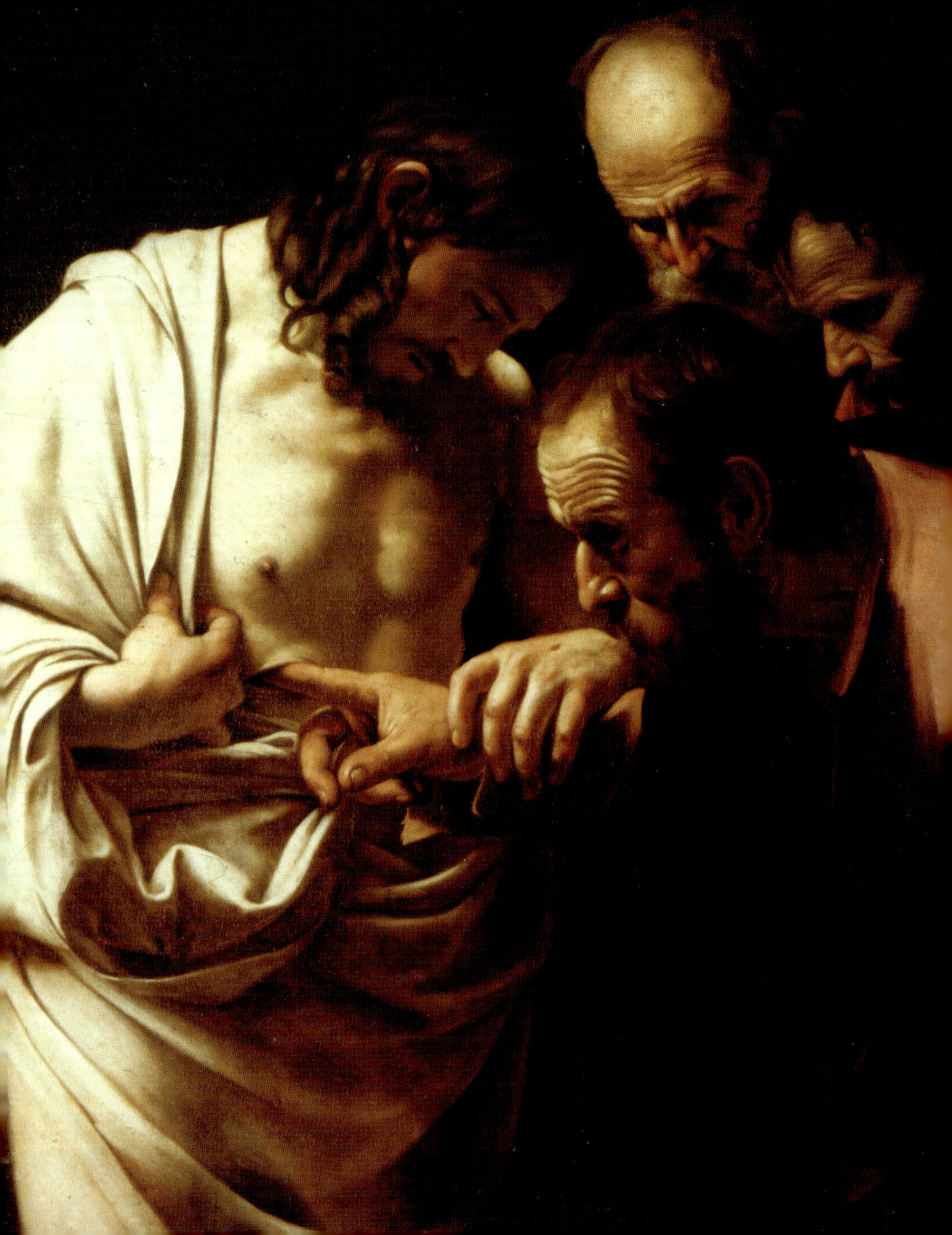

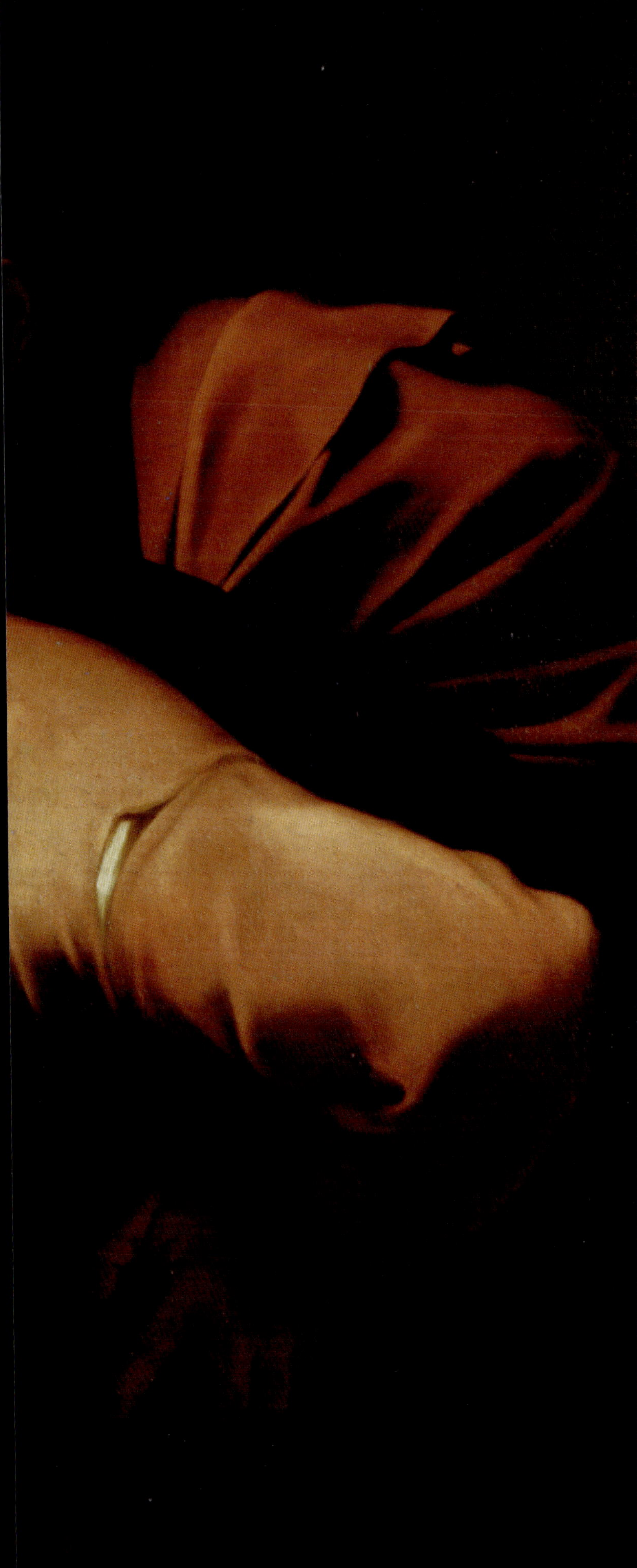

GOD'S WAYS ARE HIGHER THAN man's ways. We, as his children, barely understand the minutia of the multiplication tables of human existence, let alone the calculus of the cosmos. God could tell us neither how he brought to pass the Creation nor how he made possible the reality of the Resurrection, because, in our present condition, we would not be able to understand it fully. We need not doubt the reality of the Resurrection simply because we do not understand it. We witness the constant miracle of birth; it is real, although not fully understood. The coming of a newborn child occurs under the direction of a loving Father in Heaven. So will the resurrection of everyone who has lived, who now lives, or who will yet live upon this planet.

Neal A. Maxwell, "Our Acceptance of Christ," *Ensign*, June 1984, 69

Because our Savior lives, we do not use the symbol of his death as the symbol of our faith. But what shall we use? No sign, no work of art, no representation of form is adequate to express the glory and the wonder of the Living Christ.

Gordon B. Hinckley, "The Symbol of Christ," *Ensign*, May 1975, 92

THANKS BE TO GOD FOR THE WONDER and the majesty of His eternal plan. Thank and glorify His Beloved Son, who, with indescribable suffering, gave His life on Calvary's cross to pay the debt of mortal sin. He it was who, through His atoning sacrifice, broke the bonds of death and with godly power rose triumphant from the tomb. He is our Redeemer, the Redeemer of all mankind. He is the Savior of the world. He is the Son of God, the Author of our salvation.

Gordon B. Hinckley, "The Victory Over Death," *Ensign*, May 1985, 51

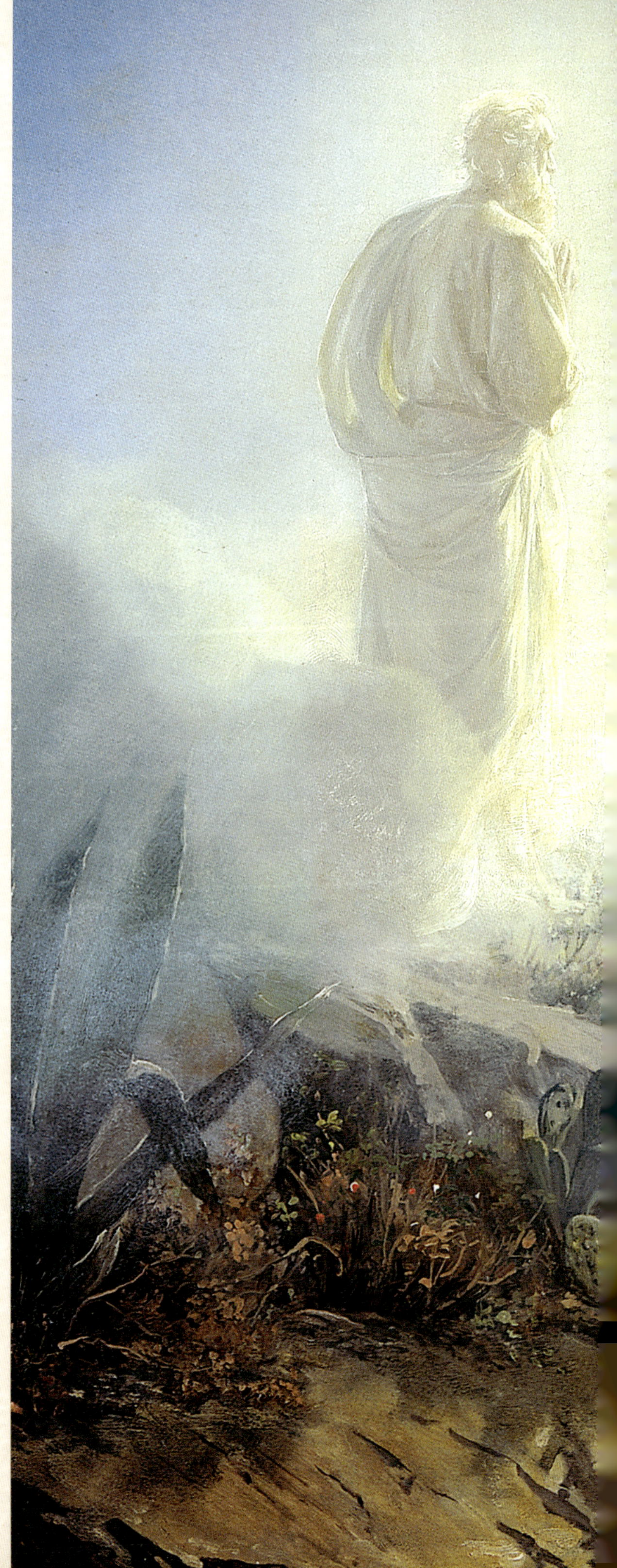

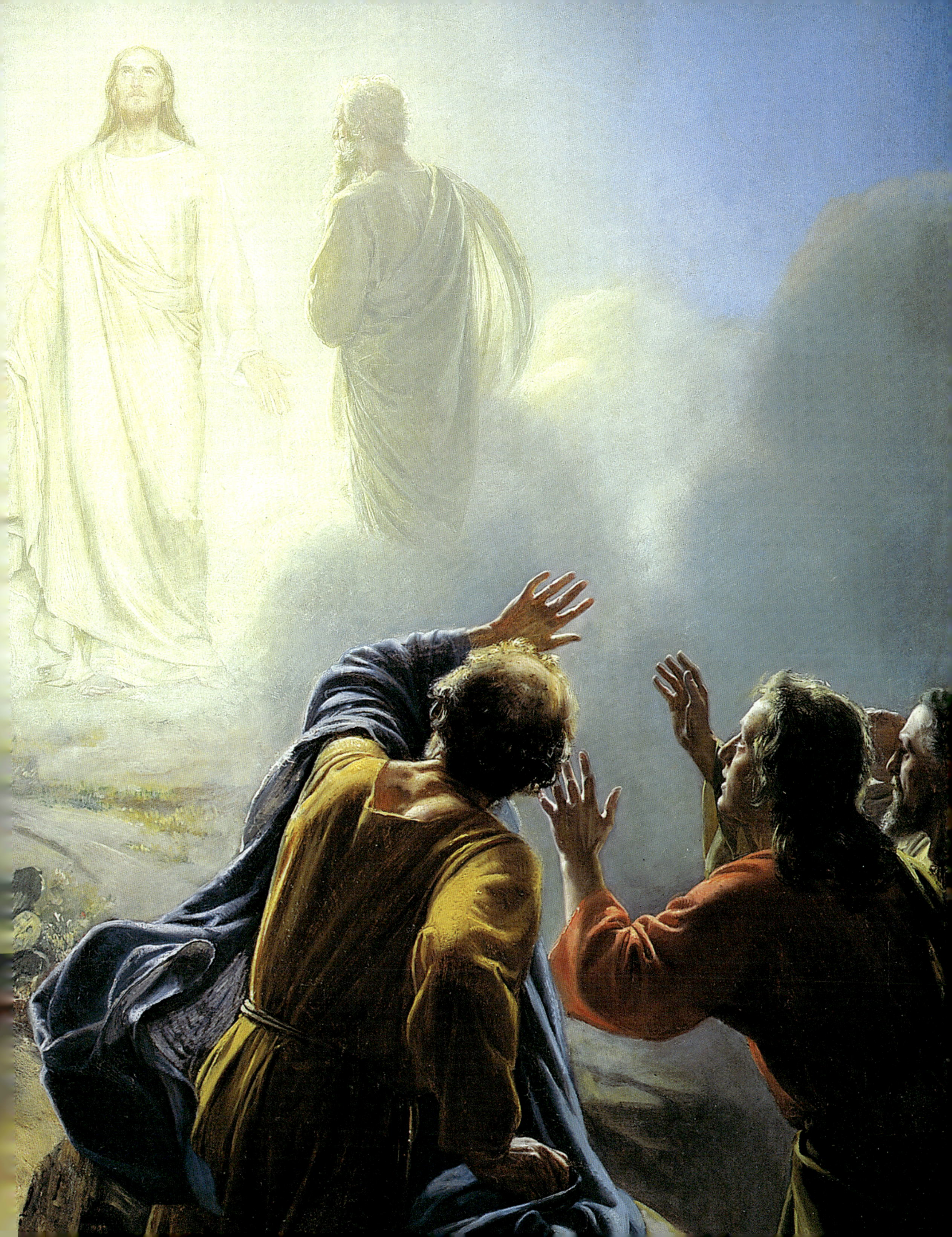

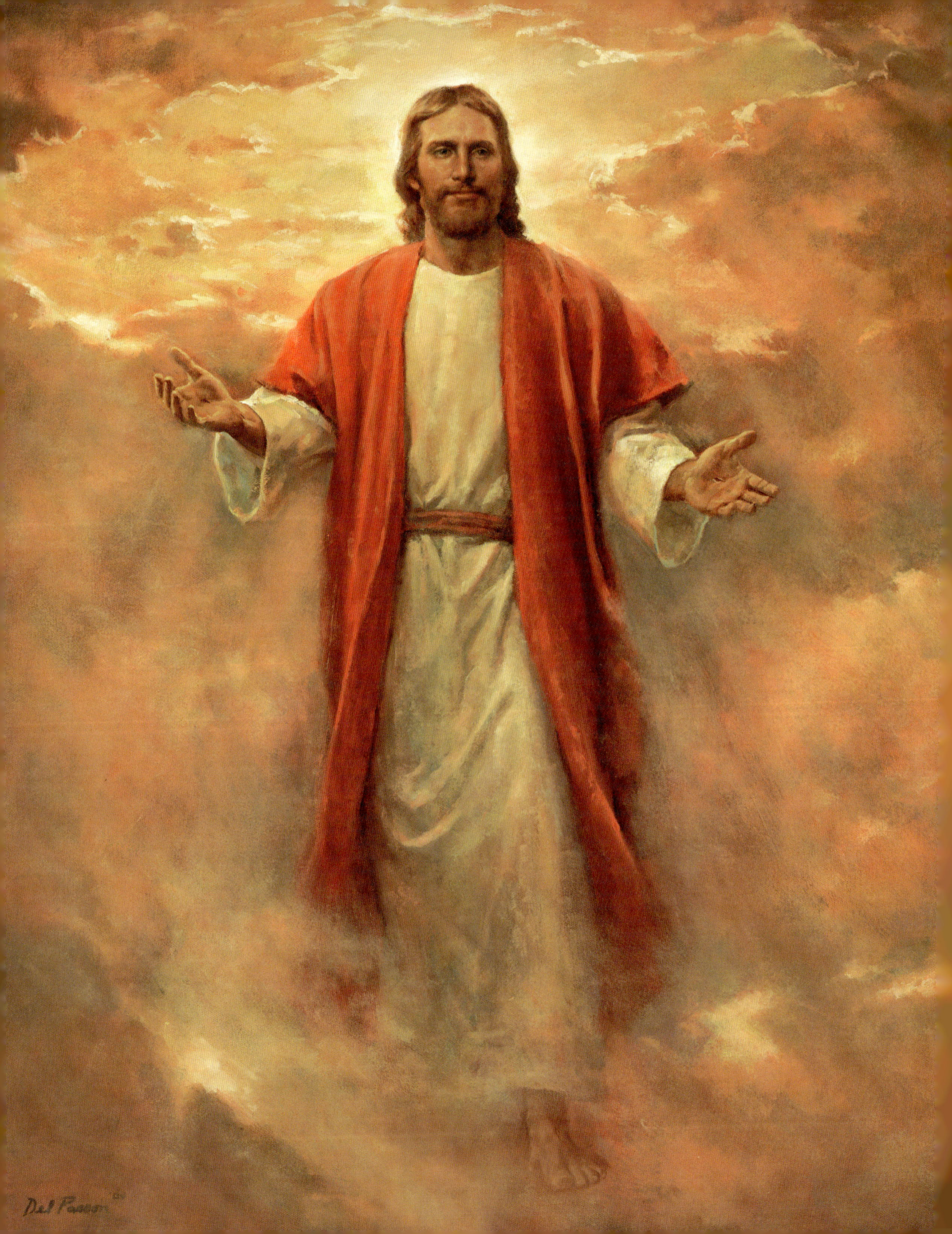
Del Parson

In the world ye shall have tribulation:
but be of good cheer;
I have overcome the world.

John 16:33

I AM THE FIRST AND THE LAST; I AM HE who liveth, I am he who was slain; I am your advocate with the Father.

D&C 110:3-4

My Work and My Glory

Our faith is centered in the true and **LIVING CHRIST,** *who is our Friend, our Lord, our God, and our King and whom we serve in worshipful adoration. We know he is God's almighty Son, that he has brought life and immortality to light through the gospel, and that all who believe in him, as he is now revealed by living prophets, shall be saved with him in the kingdom of his Father.*

Bruce R. McConkie, "The Seven Christs," *Ensign*, November 1982, 32

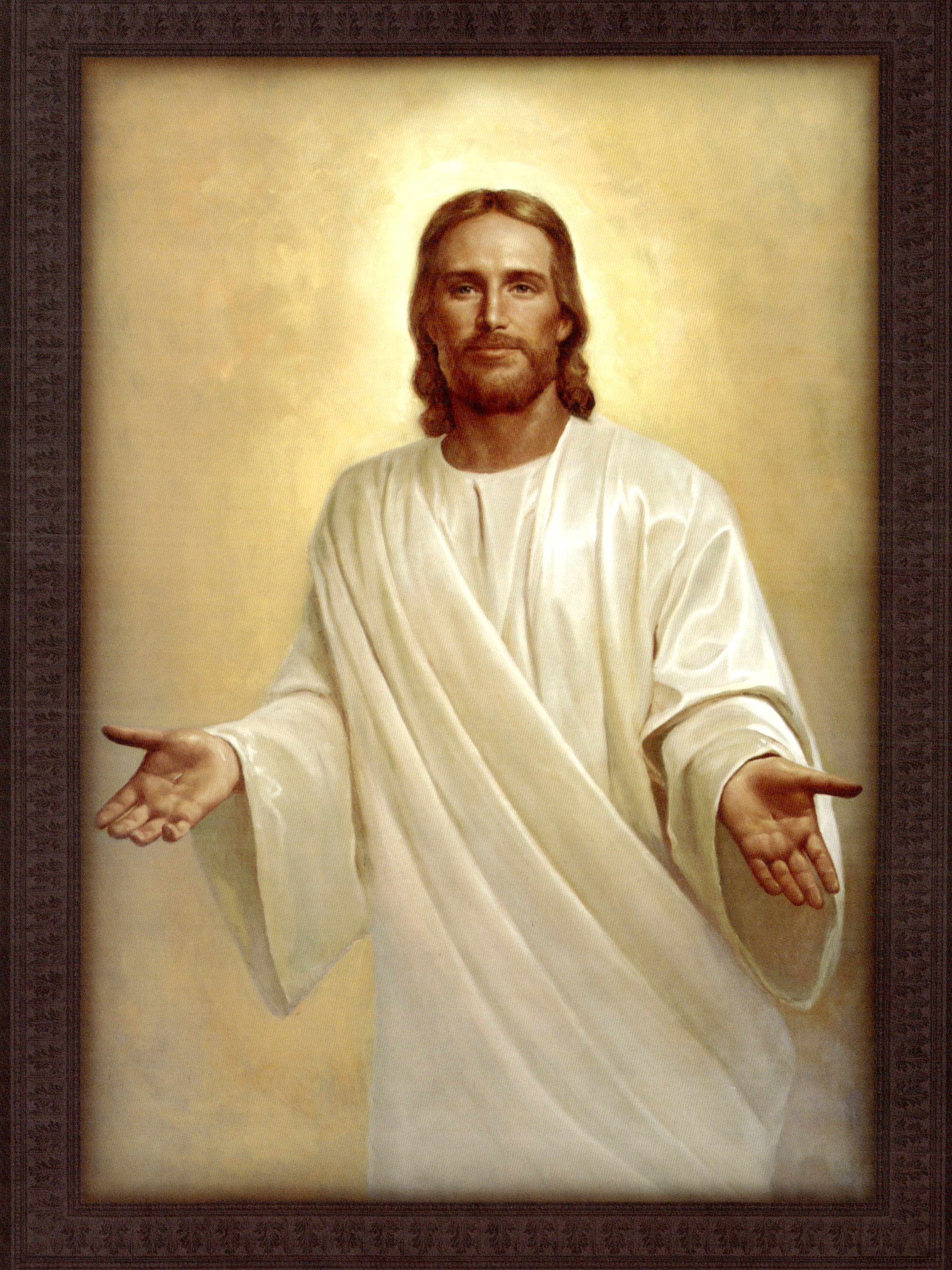

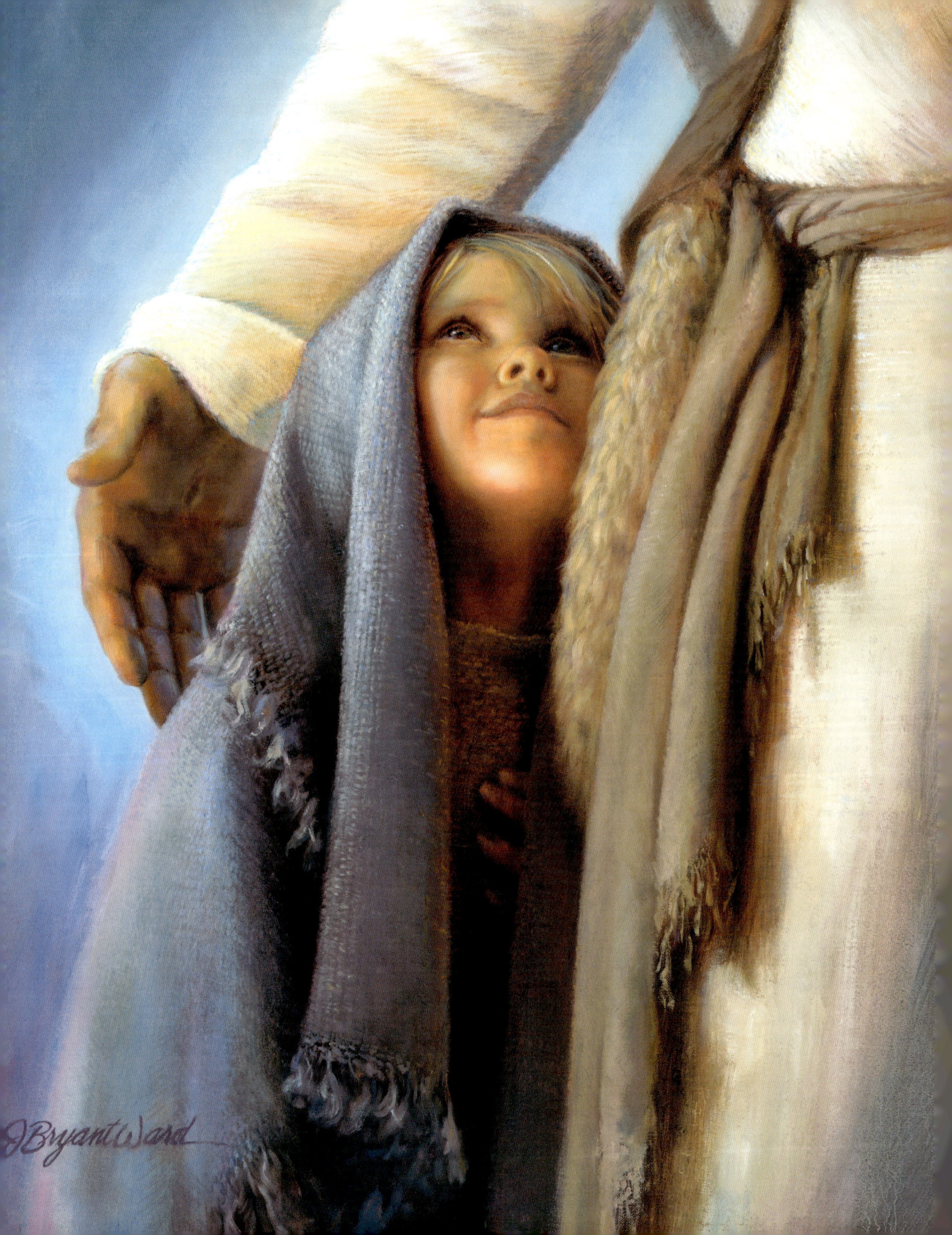
JBryantWard

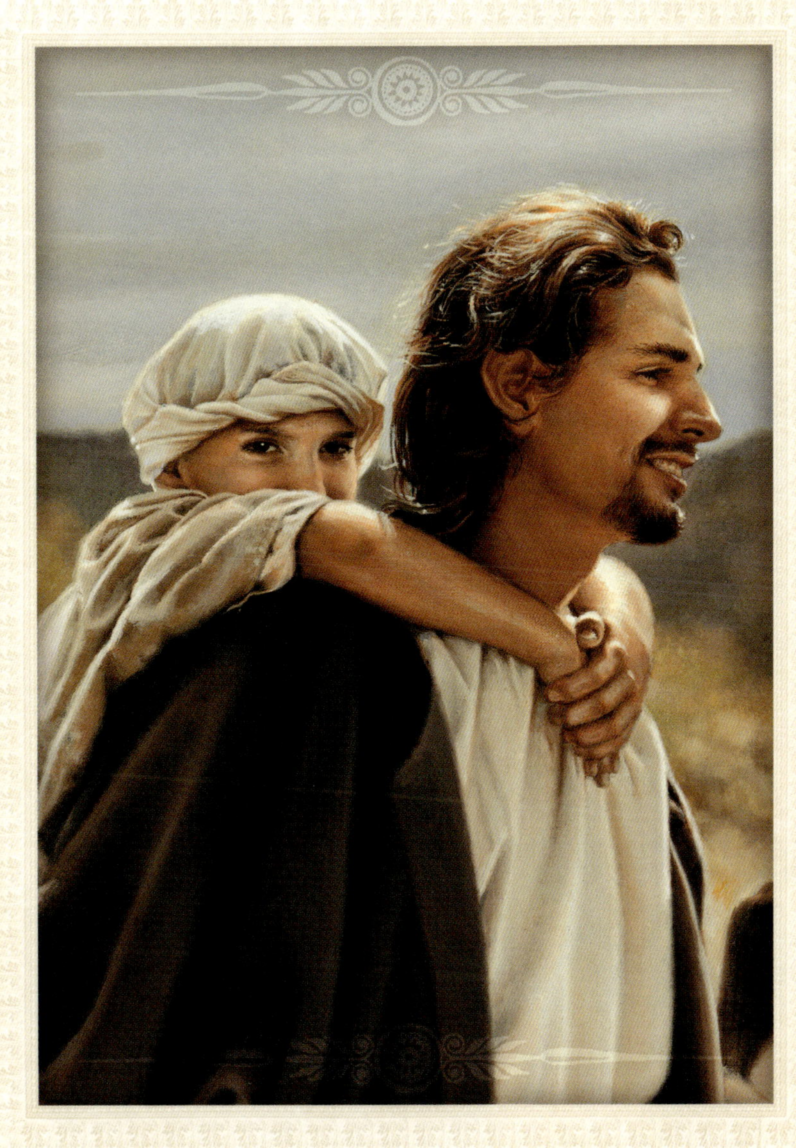

WE MIGHT ALL BE LIFTED, HELPED, EVEN CARRIED AT times by our beloved Savior, the Lord Jesus Christ. He feels what we feel; He knows our heart. It was His mission to wipe away our tears, cleanse our wounds, and bless us with His healing power. He can carry us home to our Heavenly Father with the strength of His matchless love.

Margaret D. Nadauld, "Come Unto Christ," *Ensign*, May 1998, 64

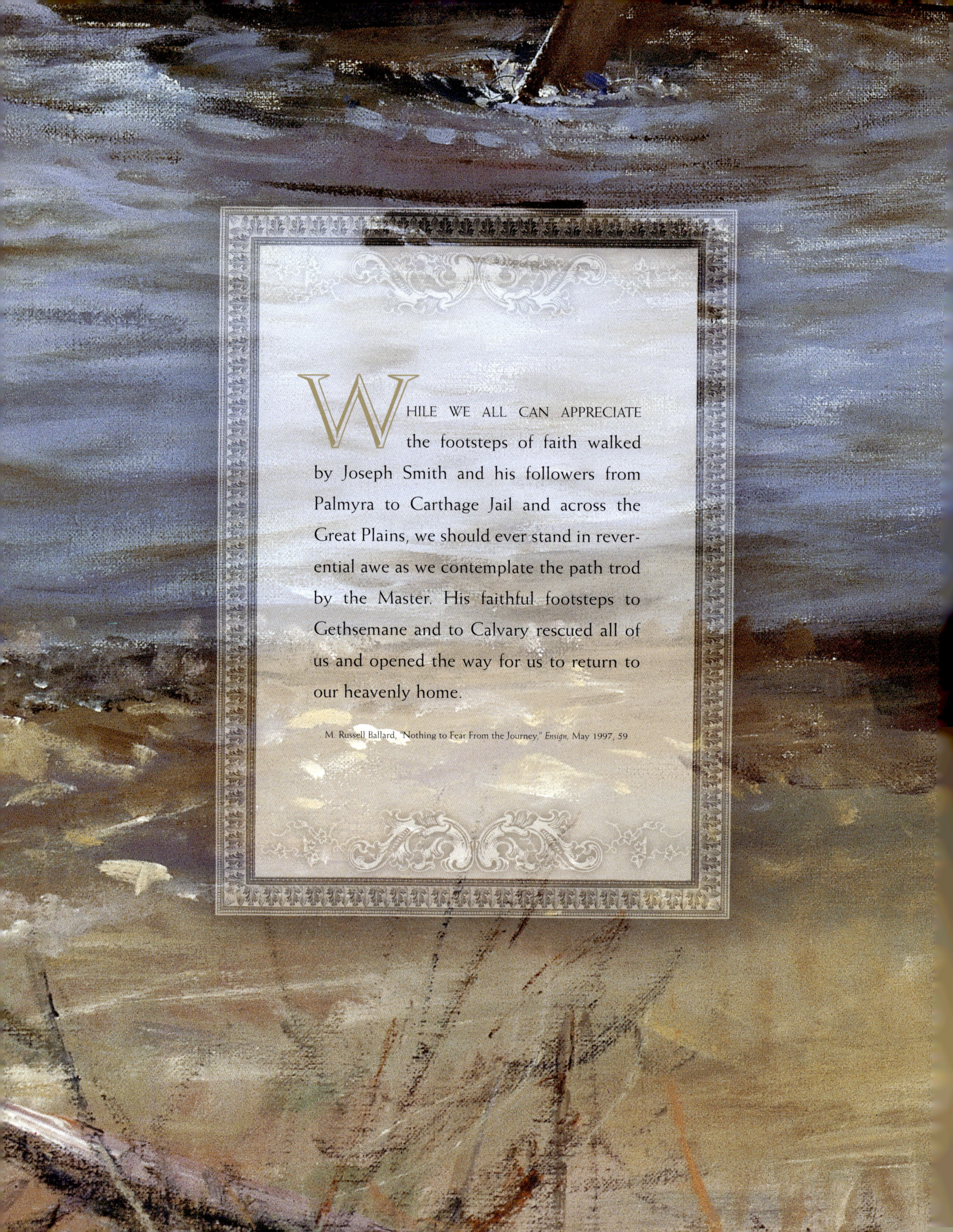

WHILE WE ALL CAN APPRECIATE the footsteps of faith walked by Joseph Smith and his followers from Palmyra to Carthage Jail and across the Great Plains, we should ever stand in reverential awe as we contemplate the path trod by the Master. His faithful footsteps to Gethsemane and to Calvary rescued all of us and opened the way for us to return to our heavenly home.

M. Russell Ballard, "Nothing to Fear From the Journey," *Ensign*, May 1997, 59

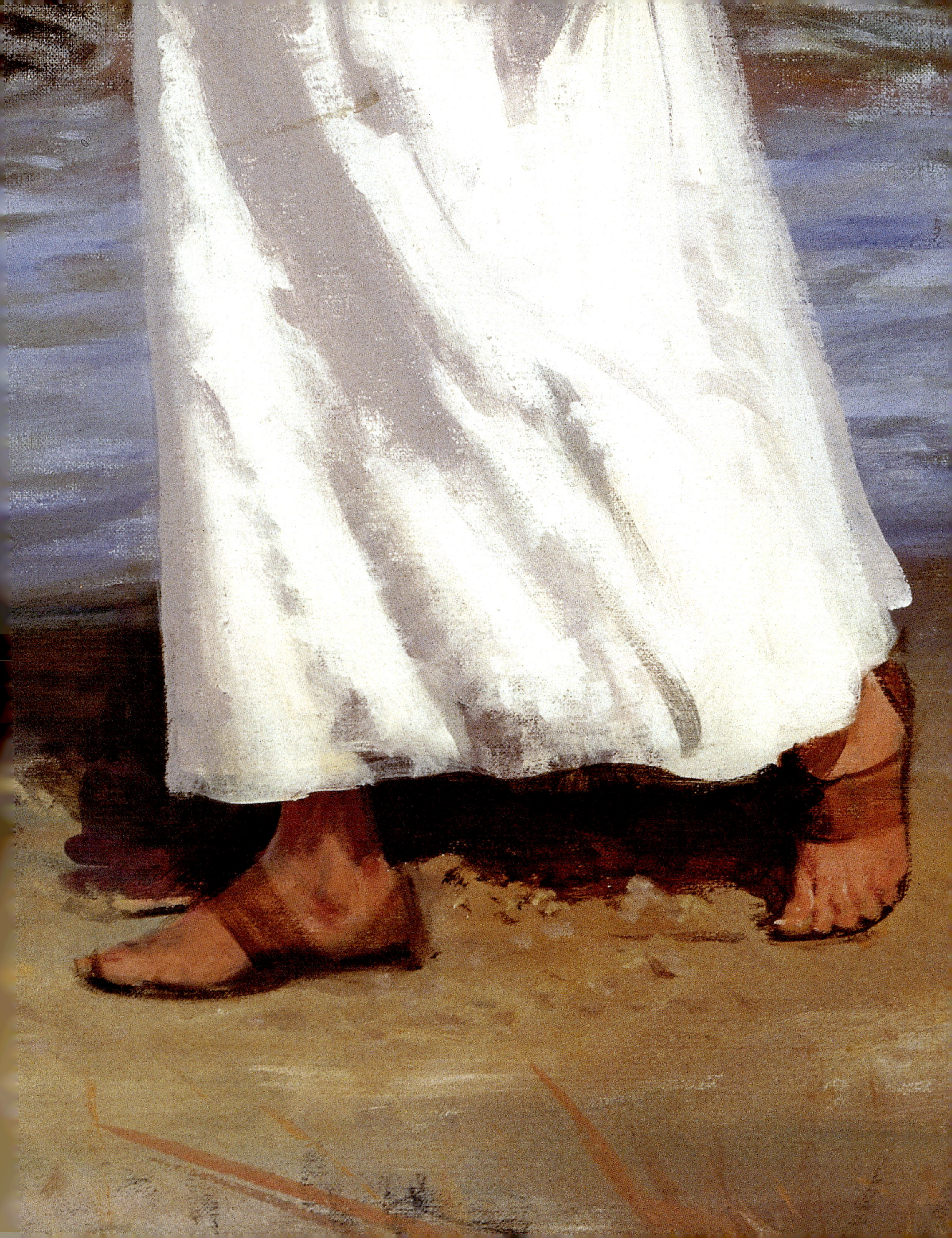

IN OUR MODERN AGE, WHERE GLORY AND fame is wrapped around medals and worldly wealth, it seems almost inconceivable to us that a solitary man, without home, without political influence, could change the course of history and eternity.

But I testify to you that He did. Jesus the Christ taught the words of life. He showed the way to truth, the way to peace, the way to happiness. I testify that when He walked the earth, thousands looked into His eyes—yearning for answers, yearning for release from suffering and grief, yearning that the burdens they carried would be lightened. Everyone who looked into His eyes with faith found healing, peace, and happiness.

As an Apostle of the Lord Jesus Christ, I testify to you this day that the time will come when every one of us will look into the Savior's loving eyes. And we will know then with a surety that a child was born to Mary who was indeed the Son of God, the Savior of the world. We will know that no grief is so great, no pain so profound, no burden so unbearable that it is beyond His healing touch.

Joseph B. Wirthlin, "Special Witnesses of Christ," *Ensign,* April 2001, 4

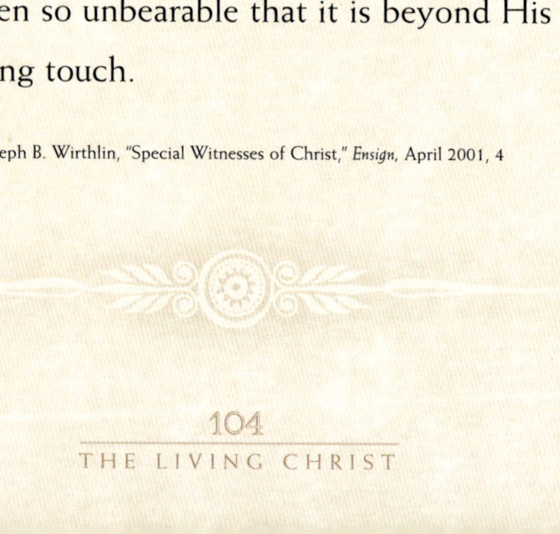

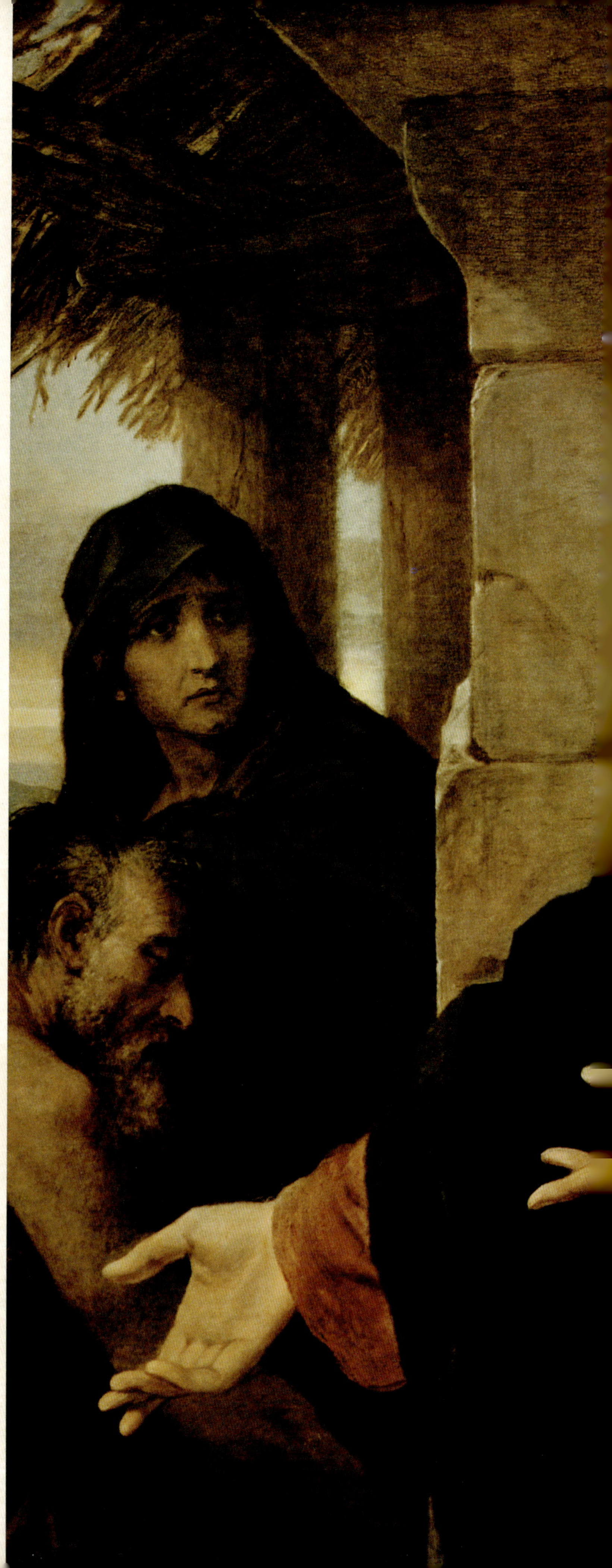

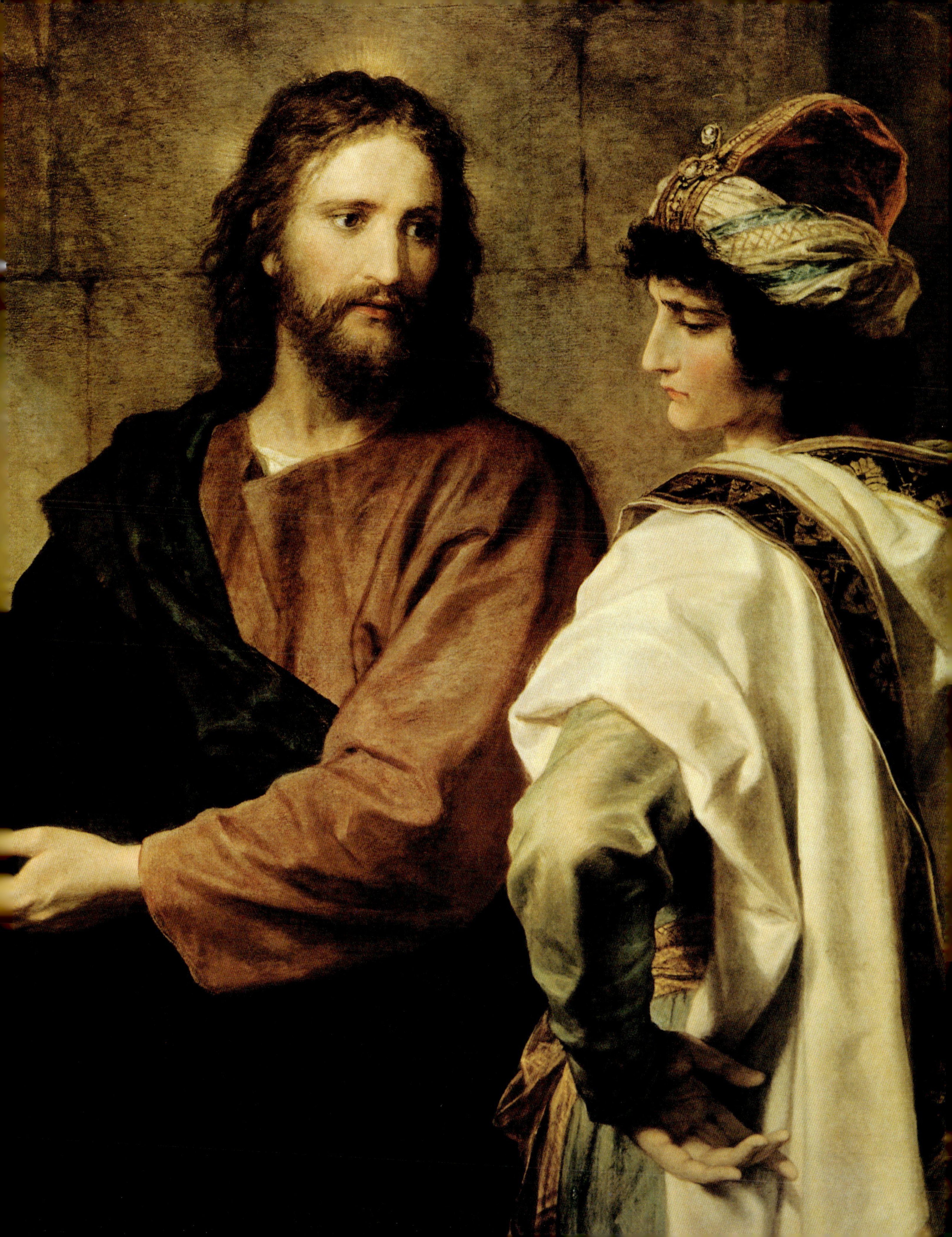

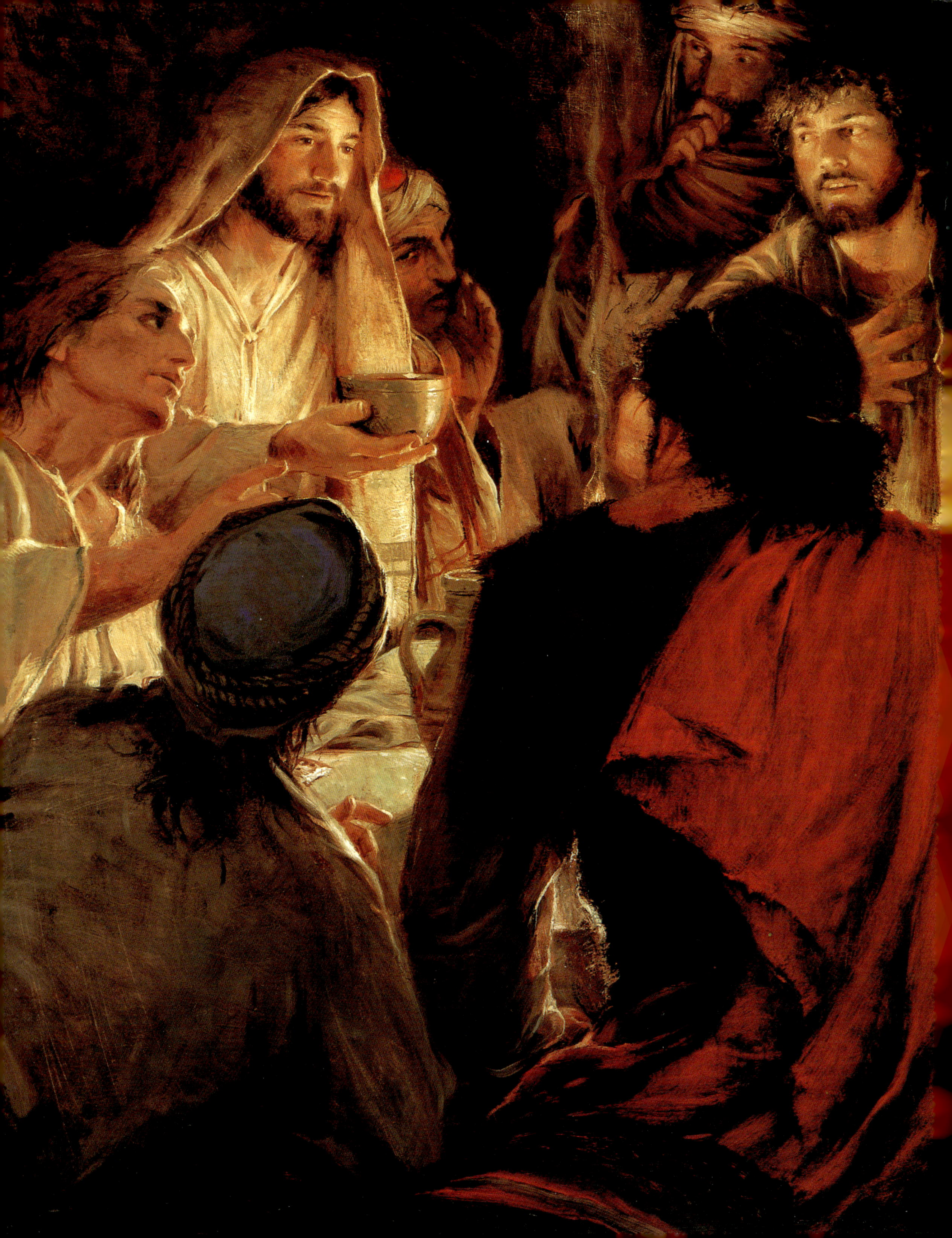

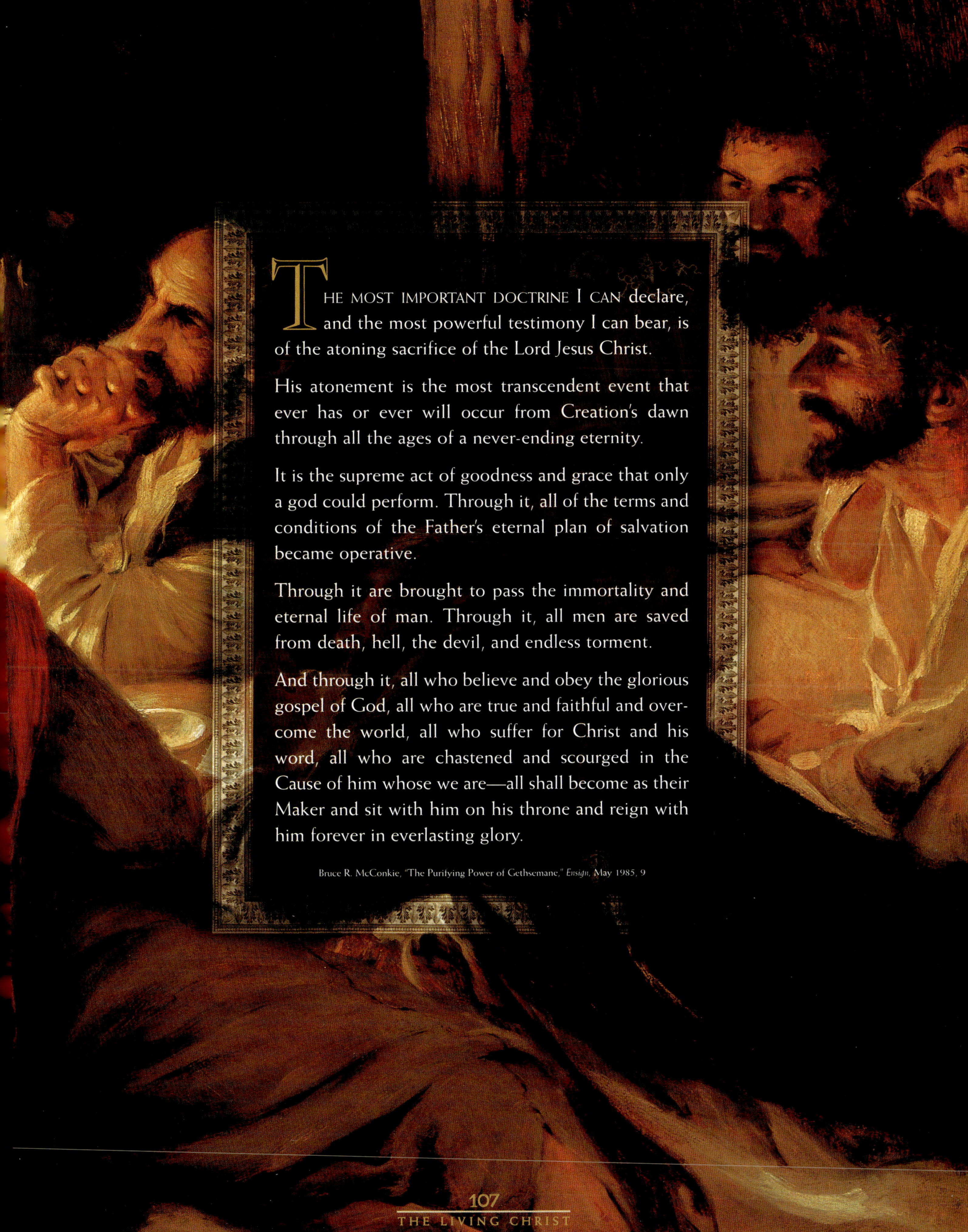

THE MOST IMPORTANT DOCTRINE I CAN declare, and the most powerful testimony I can bear, is of the atoning sacrifice of the Lord Jesus Christ.

His atonement is the most transcendent event that ever has or ever will occur from Creation's dawn through all the ages of a never-ending eternity.

It is the supreme act of goodness and grace that only a god could perform. Through it, all of the terms and conditions of the Father's eternal plan of salvation became operative.

Through it are brought to pass the immortality and eternal life of man. Through it, all men are saved from death, hell, the devil, and endless torment.

And through it, all who believe and obey the glorious gospel of God, all who are true and faithful and overcome the world, all who suffer for Christ and his word, all who are chastened and scourged in the Cause of him whose we are—all shall become as their Maker and sit with him on his throne and reign with him forever in everlasting glory.

Bruce R. McConkie, "The Purifying Power of Gethsemane," *Ensign*, May 1985, 9

And . . . I will come again,
and receive you unto myself;
that where I am, there ye may be also.

John 14:3

We knew our Heavenly Father and His Beloved Son before we came into this life. We felt peace with Them then, and we long to be with Them again, with our families and those we love.

Henry B. Eyring, "Special Witnesses of Christ," *Ensign,* April 2001, 4

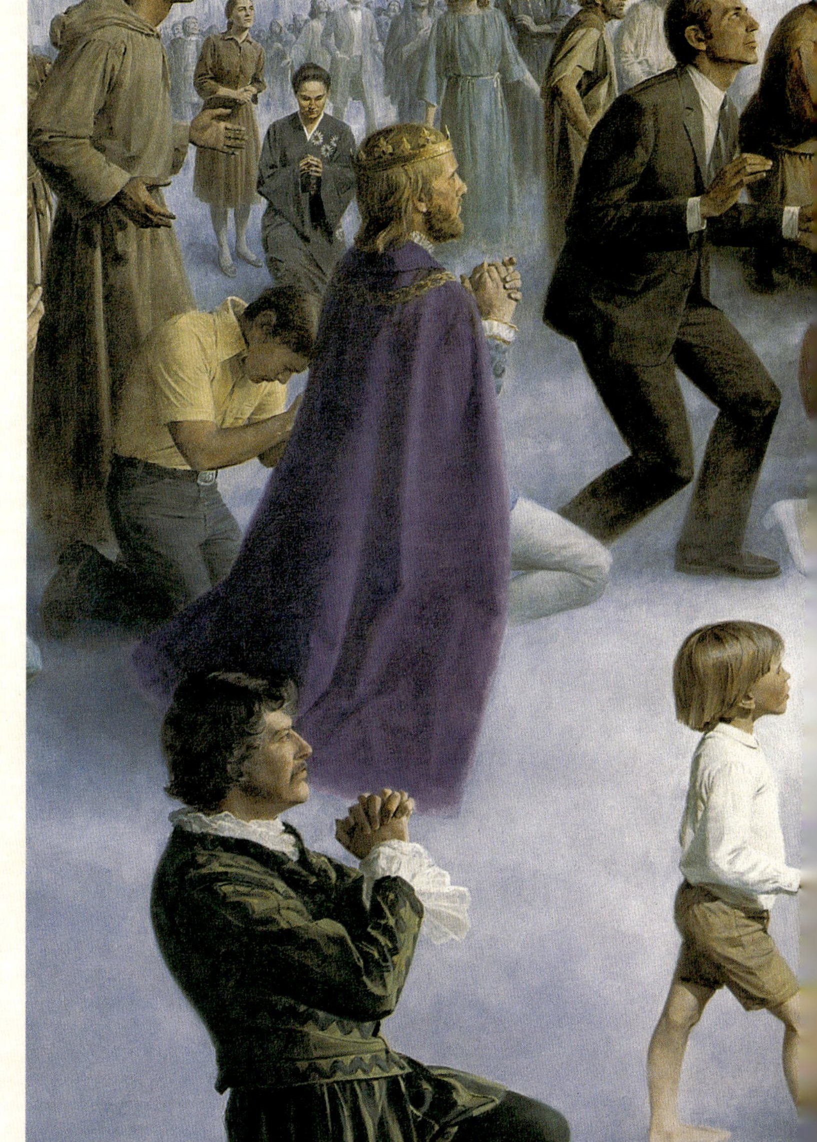

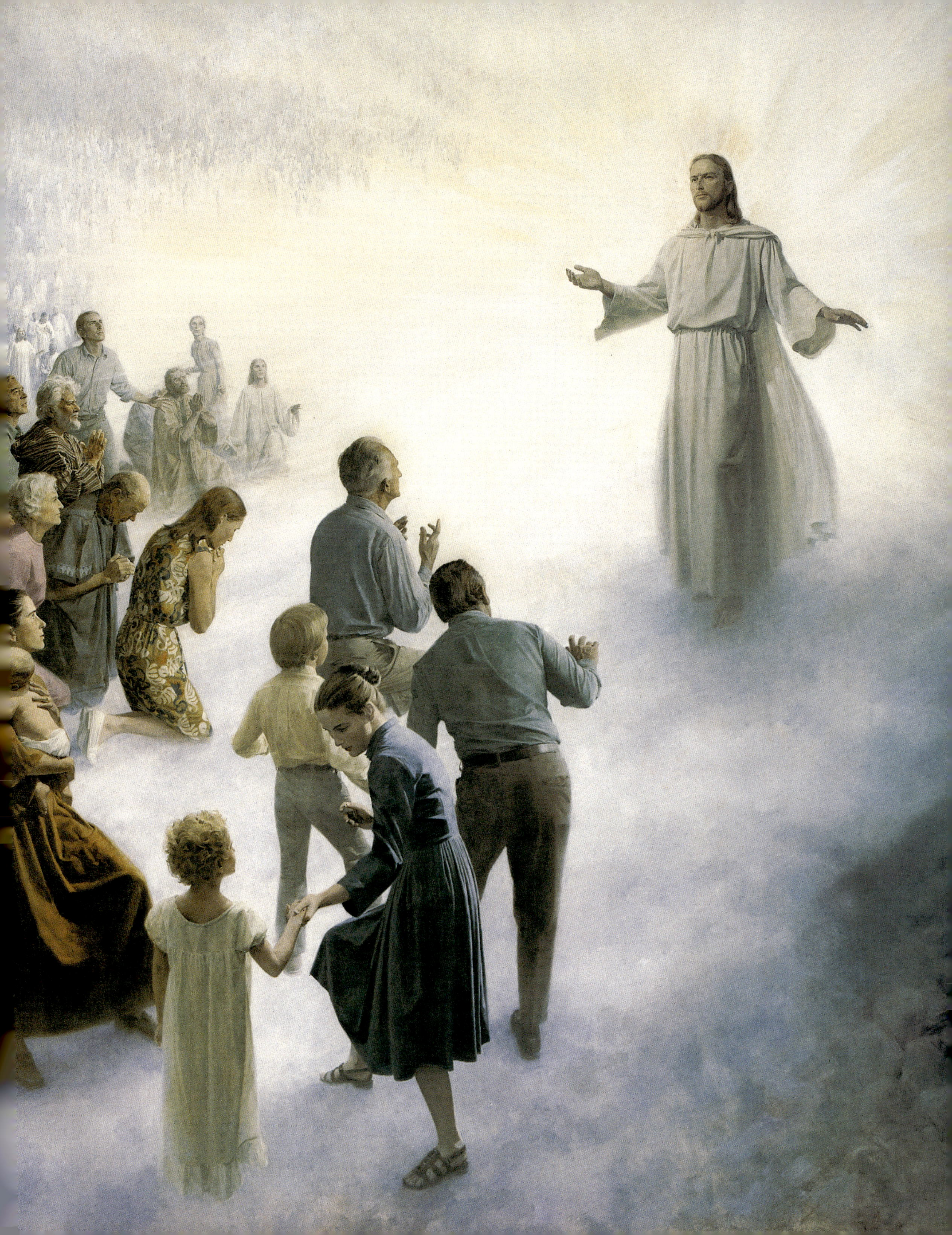

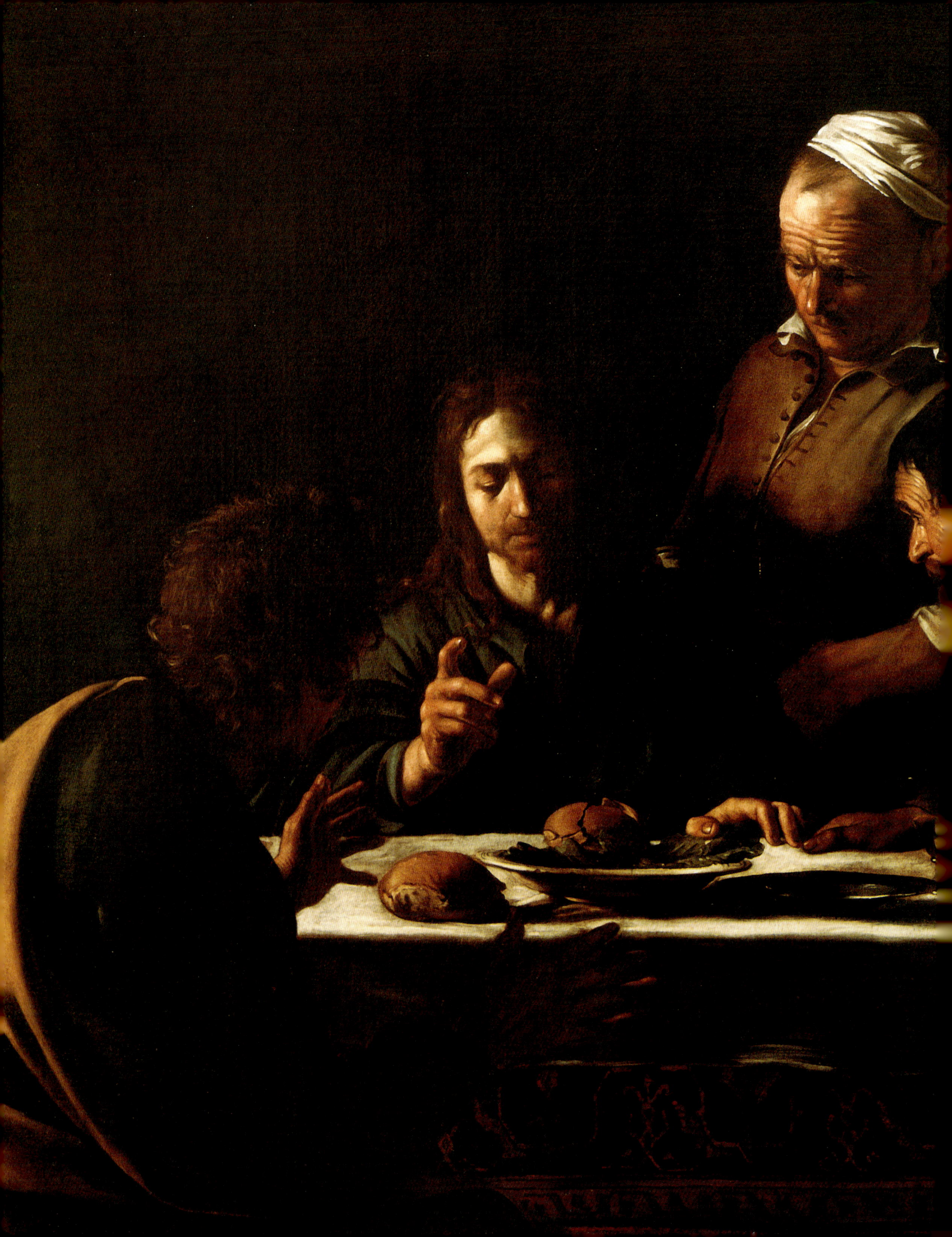

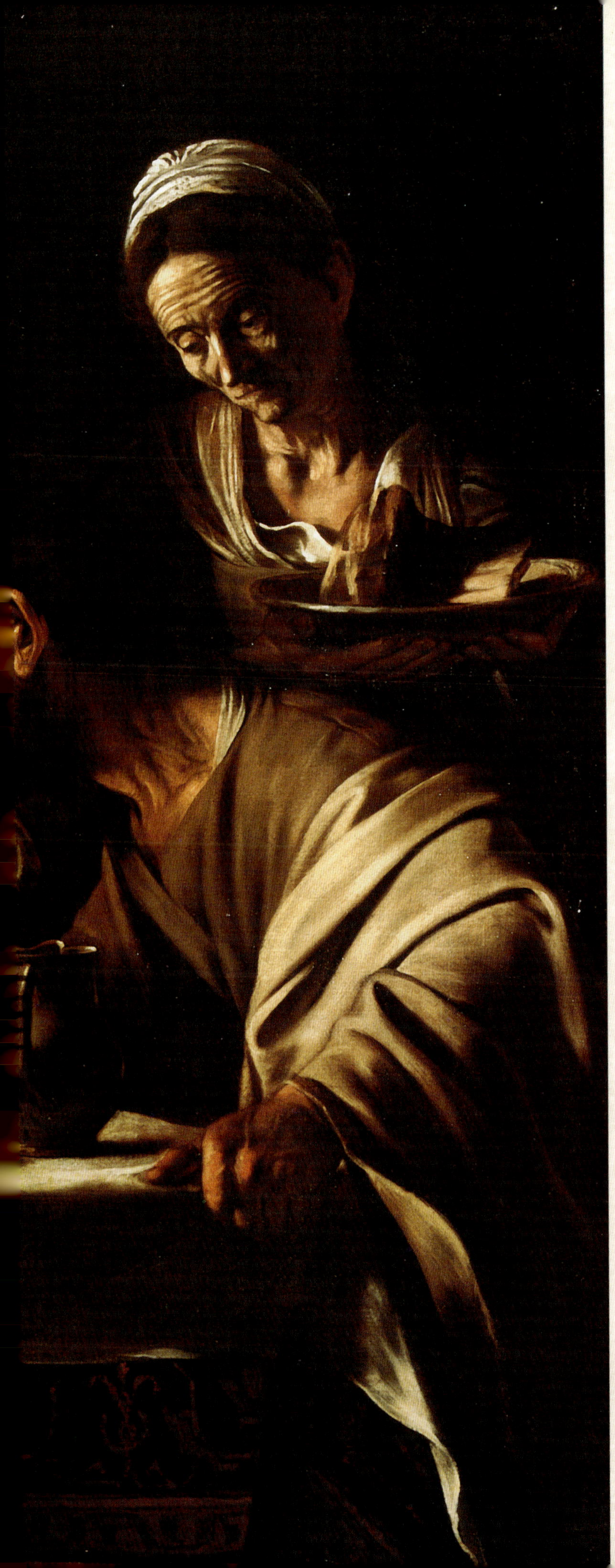

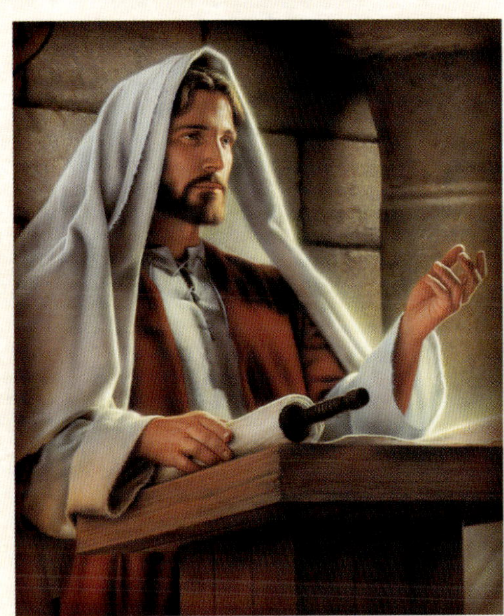

Having purchased us with His atoning blood in the great and marvelous Atonement, Jesus thereby became our Lawgiver. It is by obedience to His laws and His commandments that we may return one day to His presence and that of our Heavenly Father.

Neal A. Maxwell, "Special Witnesses of Christ," *Ensign*, April 2001, 4

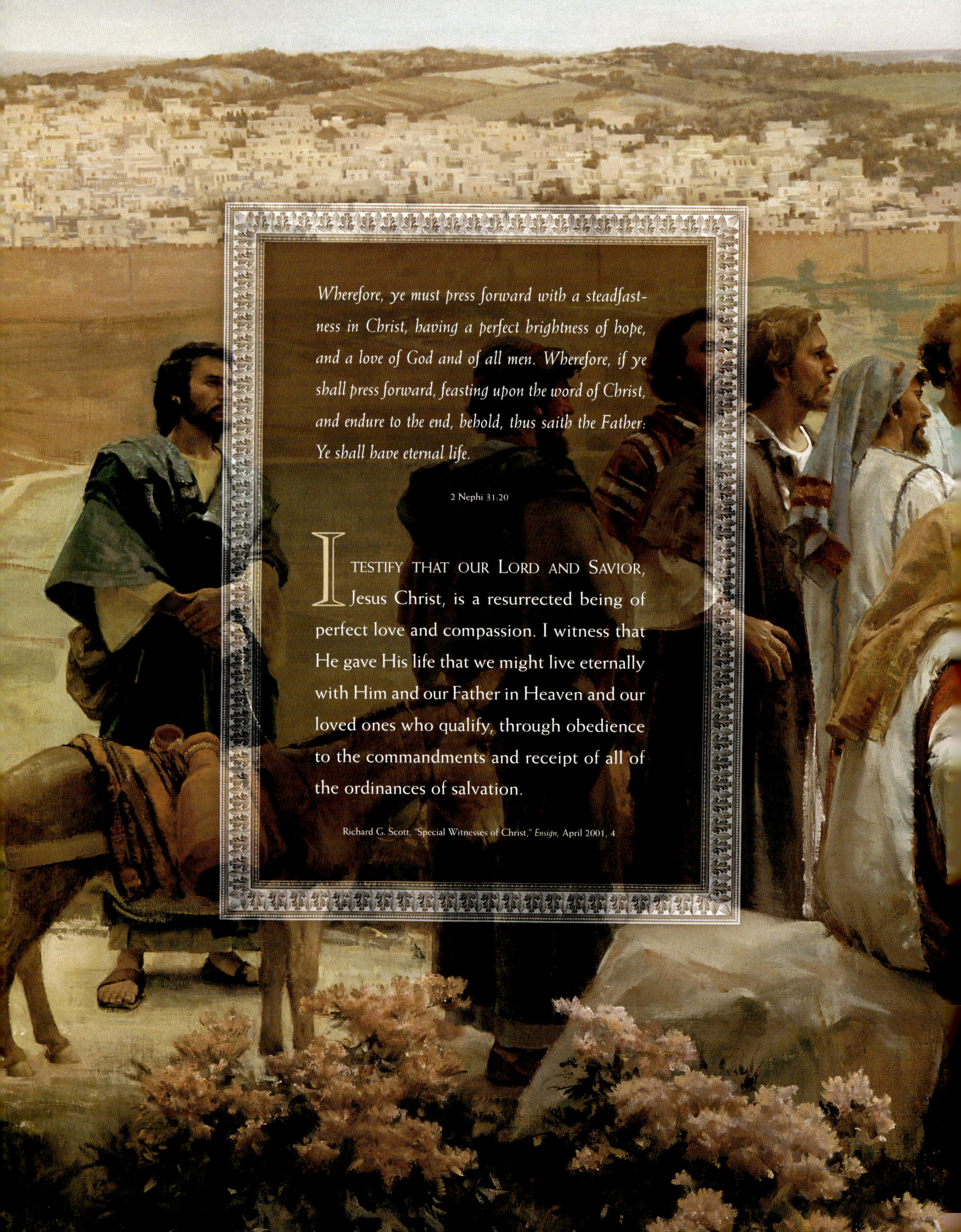

Wherefore, ye must press forward with a steadfastness in Christ, having a perfect brightness of hope, and a love of God and of all men. Wherefore, if ye shall press forward, feasting upon the word of Christ, and endure to the end, behold, thus saith the Father: Ye shall have eternal life.

2 Nephi 31:20

I testify that our Lord and Savior, Jesus Christ, is a resurrected being of perfect love and compassion. I witness that He gave His life that we might live eternally with Him and our Father in Heaven and our loved ones who qualify, through obedience to the commandments and receipt of all of the ordinances of salvation.

Richard G. Scott, "Special Witnesses of Christ," *Ensign*, April 2001, 4

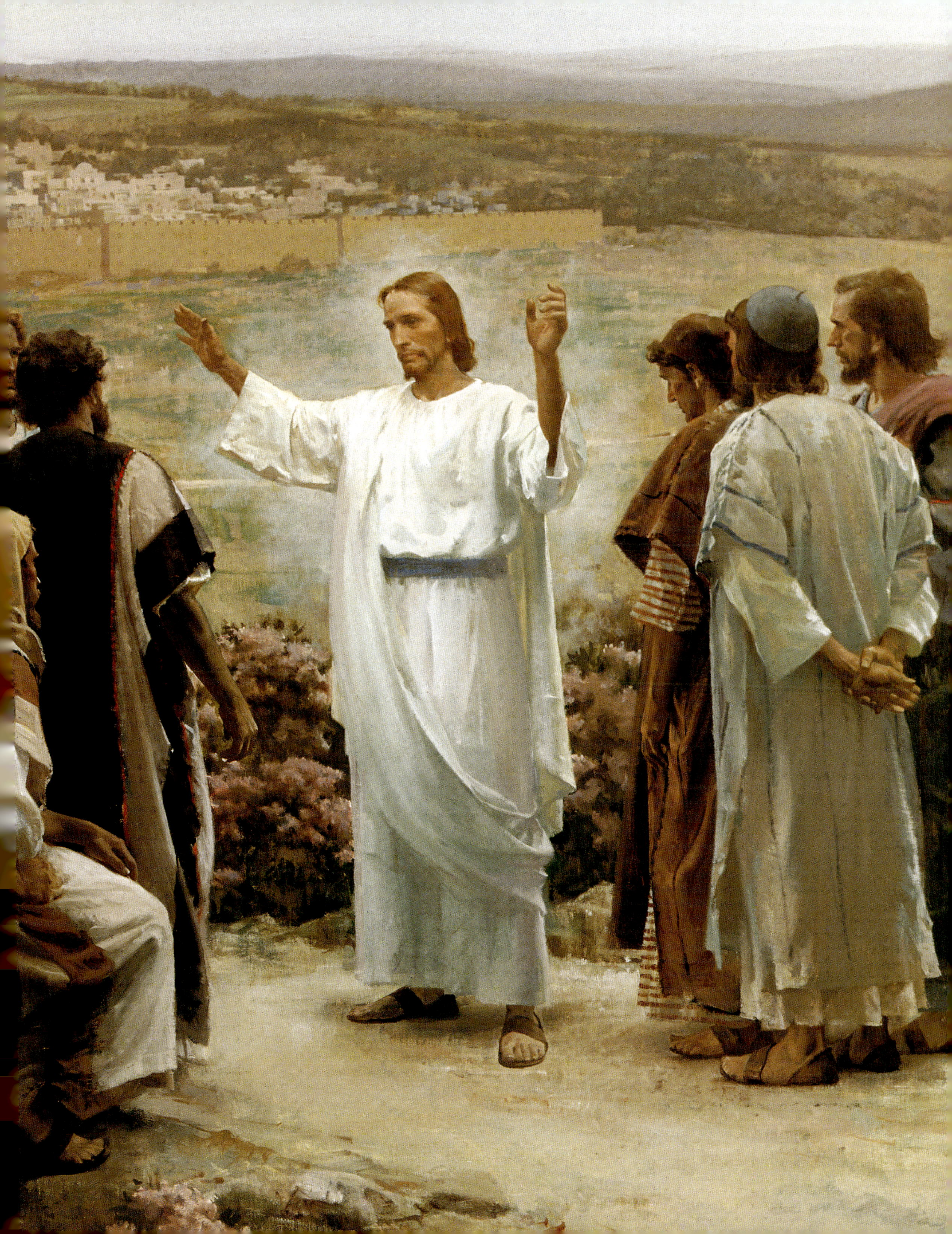

THE EARTH SHALL PASS TO ITS GLORIFIED and celestialized condition, an eternal abode for the exalted sons and daughters of God. Forever shall they reign, kings and priests to the Most High, redeemed, sanctified, and exalted through their Lord and God JESUS THE CHRIST.

James E. Talmage, *Jesus the Christ* (Salt Lake City: The Church of Jesus Christ of Latter-day Saints, 1993), 792

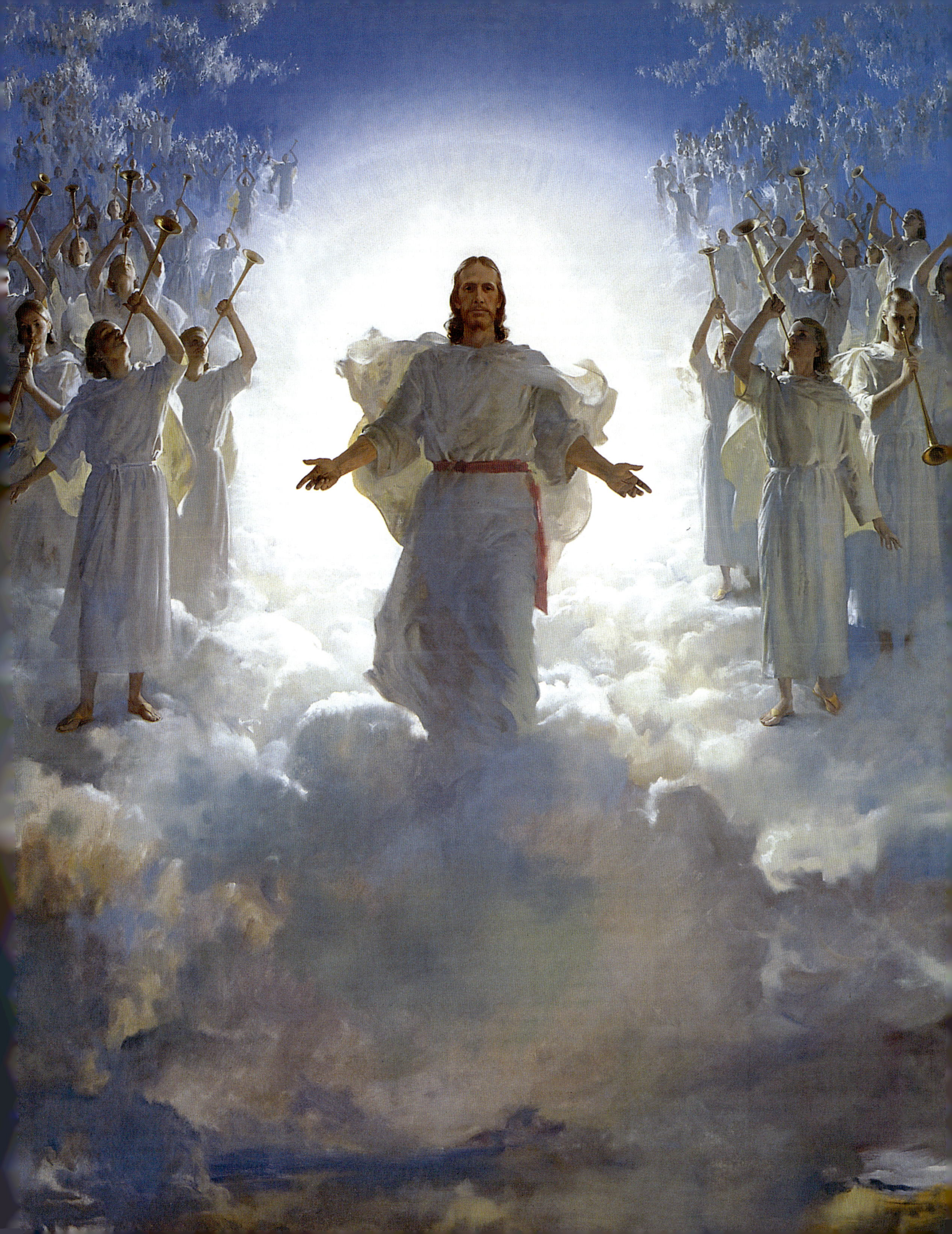

ART CREDITS

iii Cover image: *Light of the World* © 2006 Greg Olsen. Courtesy of Greg Olsen Art, LLC. For print information call 1-208-888-2585 or go to www.gregolsenart.com.

3 *Gentle Healer* by Greg Olsen © 1989 Conceptions Unlimited Investments, Inc.

5 *Forgiven* © 2006 Greg Olsen. Courtesy of Greg Olsen Art, LLC. For print information call 1-208-888-2585 or go to www.gregolsenart.com.

6 *Behold My Hands and Feet* by Harry Anderson © Intellectual Reserve, Inc. Courtesy of the Museum of Church History and Art.

7 *About My Father's Business* by Harry Anderson © Pacific Press Publishing Association, Nampa, Idaho.

8–9 *Peace, Be Still* by Arnold Friberg © Friberg Fine Art. All rights reserved. For print information go to www.fribergfineart.com.

10 *Raising of the Daughter of Jairus* © Jeffrey Hein. For more information go to www.jeffreyhein.com.

11 *Raising of Lazarus* © Jeffrey Hein. For more information go to www.jeffreyhein.com.

12 *Seeking the One* © 2006 Liz Lemon Swindle. Used with permission from Foundation Arts. For print information go to www.foundationarts.com or call 1-800-366-2781.

14–15 *Behold the Lamb of God* by Walter Rane © Intellectual Reserve, Inc. Courtesy of the Museum of Church History and Art.

15 *Hope* © Joseph F. Brickey. For more information go to www.josephbrickey.com.

16–17 *Christ Teaching the Parable of the Good Samaritan* © Robert T. Barrett.

19 *Jesus Christ* by Harry Anderson © Intellectual Reserve, Inc.

20–21 *These Twelve Jesus Sent Forth* by Walter Rane. © Intellectual Reserve, Inc. Courtesy of the Museum of Church History and Art.

23 Detail from *The First Vision* © Gary Kapp.

25 *Christ and the Boy* by Carl Heinrich Bloch. Property of Denmark government. Used courtesy of Hope Gallery. For print information go to www.hopegallery.com.

26–27 *The Bread of Life* by Roger Loveless. Courtesy of Hadley House Licensing, Minnesota, and Roger Loveless. © Roger Loveless/Hadley House 2006.

28–29 *Sermon on the Mount* by Harry Anderson © Intellectual Reserve, Inc. Courtesy of the Museum of Church History and Art.

31 Detail from *The Transfiguration* © 2006 Greg Olsen. Courtesy of Greg Olsen Art, LLC. For print information call 1-208-888-2585 or go to www.gregolsenart.com.

32–33 *Jehovah Creates the Earth* by Walter Rane © Intellectual Reserve, Inc. Courtesy of the Museum of Church History and Art.

34 *As I Have Loved You* © 2006 Simon Dewey. Courtesy of Altus Fine Art. www.altusfineart.com.

36–37 *Behold the Man* © 2006 Simon Dewey. Courtesy of Altus Fine Art. www.altusfineart.com.

39 *Son of Man* © J. Kirk Richards. For more information go to www.jkirkrichards.com.

40–41 *Christ Teaching Mary and Martha* by Anton Dorph. Used courtesy of Hope Gallery. For print information go to www.hopegallery.com

43 *Christ in Prayer and Meditation* © Michael J. Nelson.

44–45 *Well of Life* © Robert T. Barrett.

46 *Atonement* © Patrick Devonas. For print information contact pdevonas@juno.com.

48–49 *Christ Healing the Sick at the Pool of Bethesda* by Carl Heinrich Bloch. Courtesy of Brigham Young University Museum of Art. All rights reserved. Uncropped image shown here:

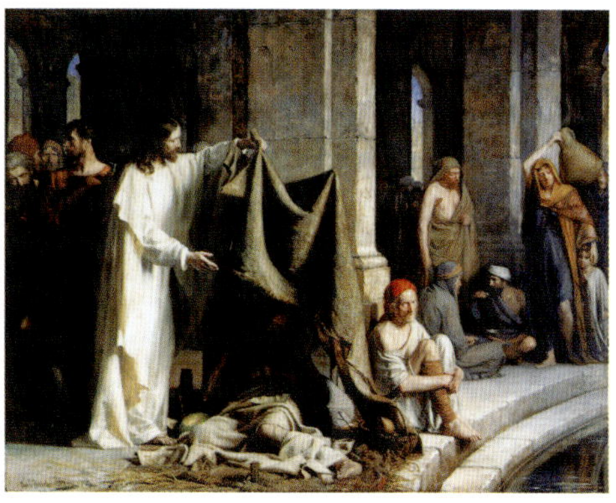

50 *Triumphal Entry* © Walter Rane. Courtesy of the Stable Gallery. 801-355-6872.

52–53 *Christ Calling to the Disciples* © David Lindsley.

53 *Lovest Thou Me More Than These?* © David Lindsley.

54–55 *Approaching Storm* by Roger Loveless. Courtesy of Hadley House Licensing, Minnesota, and Roger Loveless. © Roger Loveless/Hadley House 2006.

56 *The Good Shepherd* © Greg Olsen. Courtesy of Greg Olsen Art, LLC. For print information call 1-208-888-2585 or go to www.gregolsenart.com.

59 *Divine Redeemer* © 2006 Simon Dewey. Courtesy of Altus Fine Art. www.altusfineart.com

60 *Christ Being Taken From the Cross* © Walter Rane. Courtesy of the Stable Gallery. 801-355-6872.

61 *He That Is Without Sin* © Walter Rane. Courtesy of the Bainbridge Island Ward, Bainbridge Island, Washington.

62–63 *In Humility* © 2006 Simon Dewey. Courtesy of Altus Fine Art. www.altusfineart.com.

64 *Not My Will, But Thine* by Harry Anderson © Pacific Press Publishing Association, Nampa, Idaho.

66–67 *The Hour Is at Hand* © Walter Rane. Courtesy of the Stable Gallery. 801-355-6872.

68 *Flagellation de Notre Seigneur Jésus Christ (The Flagellation of Our Lord Jesus Christ)* by William Bouguereau, courtesy of the collection of Fine Arts photography Cathedral of La Rochelle, La Rochelle, France. Photographer J+M

Numerique. Used by permission. All rights reserved.

70 *The Messiah* © Patrick Devonas. From the collection of David & Karen Lynn Davidson. For print information contact pdevonas@juno.com.

70–71 *Grey Day Golgotha* © J. Kirk Richards. For print information go to www.jkirkrichards.com.

72–73 *L' Enterrement du Christ (The Burial of Christ)* by Antonio Cesari.

75 *Christ in Gethsemane* by Heinrich Hofmann. © C. Harrison Conroy and Co., Inc. All rights reserved.

76 *For Unto Us a Child is Born* © 2006 Simon Dewey. Courtesy of Altus Fine Art. www.altusfineart.com.

77 *Christ With Crown of Thorns and Staff* etching by Carl Heinrich Bloch. Used courtesy of Hope Gallery. For print information www.hopegallery.com.

78–79 *Jesus Christ Visits the Americas* by John Scott © Intellectual Reserve, Inc. Courtesy of the Museum of Church History and Art.

80 *Living Water* by Roger Loveless. Courtesy of Hadley House Licensing, Minnesota, and Roger Loveless. © Roger Loveless/Hadley House 2006.

83 Detail from *The Doubtful Thomas* by Carl Heinrich Bloch. Used courtesy of Hope Gallery. For print information go to www.hopegallery.com.

84 *Blind Man Healed* sketch © 2006 Liz Lemon Swindle. Used with permission from Foundation Arts. For print information go to www.foundation-arts.com or call 1-800-366-2781.

85 *Christ Healing the Blind* © Jeffrey Hein. For more information go to www.jeffreyhein.com.

86–87 *Christ Walking on the Waters* by Sergius Julius Von Klever. Courtesy of Sotheby's Picture Library, London. For information on art prints go to www.foveditions.com.

89 *The Resurrection of Jesus Christ* © Patrick Devonas. From the collection of Michael Huffington. For print information contact pdevonas@juno.com.

90 *He Is Risen* © 2006 Simon Dewey. Courtesy of Altus Fine Art. www.altusfineart.com.

92–93 *The Incredulity of Saint Thomas* by Michelangelo Merisi da Caravaggio, courtesy of Prussian Palaces and Gardens Foundation Berlin-Brandenburg. Used by permission. All rights reserved.

94–95 *The Transfiguration* by Carl Heinrich Bloch. Courtesy of Det Nationalhistoriske Museum på Frederiksborg, Hillerød.

96 *In His Glory* © Del Parson. For more information go to www.delparson.com.

99 *Welcome* © Del Parson. For more information go to www.delparson.com.

100 *Under His Wing* © Jay Bryant Ward. By arrangement with Mill Pond Press, Inc. Venice, FL 34292. For information on art prints by Jay Ward, please contact Mill Pond Press 1-800-535-0331.

101 *Hold On Tight* © 2006 Liz Lemon Swindle. Used with permission from Foundation Arts. For print information go to www.foundationarts.com or call 1-800-366-2781.

102–3 Detail from *Christ Calling Peter & Andrew* by Harry Anderson © Intellectual Reserve, Inc. Courtesy of the Museum of Church History and Art.

104–5 *Christ with the Rich Young Ruler* by Heinrich Hofman © C. Harrison Conroy and Co., Inc. All rights reserved.

106–7 *Peace I Give unto You* © Walter Rane. Courtesy of the Stable Gallery. 801-355-6872.

108–9 *The Last Judgment of Jesus Christ* by John Scott © Intellectual Reserve, Inc.

110–11 *Supper at Emmaus* by Michelangelo Merisi da Caravaggio. Milan, Pinacoteca di Brera. Under license from Italian Ministry for Cultural Goods and Activities.

111 *Light and Truth* © 2006 Simon Dewey. Courtesy of Altus Fine Art. www.altusfineart.com.

112–13 *Go Ye Therefore and Teach* by Harry Anderson © Intellectual Reserve, Inc. Courtesy of the Museum of Church History and Art.

115 *The Second Coming* by Harry Anderson © Intellectual Reserve, Inc. Courtesy of the Museum of Church History and Art.